PERSO-ARABIC HYBRIDS IN HINDI

THE SOCIO-LINGUISTIC AND STRUCTURAL ANALYSIS

Perso-Arabic Hybrids in Hindi

THE SOCIO-LINGUISTIC AND STRUCTURAL ANALYSIS

AGNIESZKA KUCZKIEWICZ-FRAŚ

MANOHAR
2003

The book was financially supported by the Institute of Oriental Philology and by the Philological Faculty, Jagiellonian University, Kraków, Poland.

The author is a beneficiary of the Foundation for Polish Science.

First published 2003

ISBN 81-7304-498-8

Published by
Ajay Kumar Jain for
Manohar Publishers & Distributors
4753/23 Ansari Road, Daryaganj
New Delhi 110002

Printed at
Lordson Publishers Pvt Ltd
Delhi 110007

For Jarek, Felix and Mieszko
with love

Contents

INTRODUCTION

From the very beginning of its existence Hindi has been a subject for foreign influences. Close contact with Persian brought to India by Muslim invaders, lasting for several centuries, has borne fruit in the form of an enormous quantity of borrowings of different types. In the case of Persian and Hindi we can observe the whole process of enriching one language by the elements of the other.

The very first stage was the borrowing of simple, everyday words. That is often connected with adopting the new objects they denote. Thus, such Persian and Arabic words, as: *k̲alam* 'pen', *kāgaz* 'paper', *masjid* 'mosque', *huk̲k̲ā* 'water-pipe', *darvāzā* 'door', *darbār* 'a royal court', *k̲h̲ānā* 'house', *dukān* 'shop', *āsmān* 'sky', *zamīn* 'earth', *dost* 'friend', *duśman* 'enemy', and many, many other, have appeared in Hindi.

In the course of time, these borrowed words have naturalised in Hindi, becoming a regular part of the Hindi lexis and subject to the grammatical system of the borrowing language (cf. inflexional hybridisation described in the Chapter III.4.). They started being employed as parts of compounds – so widely used in Hindi – joining the native words and forming the simplest possible hybrid forms (**hybrids of type 1**, see p. 71 ff.).

They have also undergone the morphological patterns of the borrowing language, taking its inflexions as well as formatives (**hybrids of type 2**, see p. 76-77.).

The last stage in the chain of the borrowing processes is creating hybrid words with native (in our case Hindi) bases and borrowed (in this case Persian or Arabic) affixes (**hybrids of type 3**, see p. 77 ff.). The obvious fact is that derivational affixes are not borrowed as such – they occur as an integral part of various whole loan-words and can be borrowed only when occuring in enough foreign words. This type of hybrid words in Hindi is the main subject of this book, although types 1 and 2, for their undisputed importance, have also been discussed (cf. Chapters III.3. and III.4.).

The existence of hybrid words (especially of type 3) in a language proves the full assimilation of foreign elements borrowed by this language. Studying them helps answer the question of productivity of assimilated formatives and of the level of grammatical permeability of the borrowing tongue. The quality and common usage of hybrid words show how deeply and organically the initially strange, Perso-Arabic vocabulary, has blended into the tissue of Hindi. The assimilated Perso-Arabic bases and formatives have supplied the stock of Indian word-formatting elements, assuming equality in the whole system of Hindi word-formation, and enriching significantly the Hindi lexis.

Though hybrid words appear probably in every language, in Hindi their role is particular. They demonstrate its enormous ability for syncretising new, alien components without much harm to itself. New elements borrowed by Hindi do not replace native ones but start functioning side by side, becoming in the course of time a rightful ingredient of the whole system of Hindi.

Studying Perso-Arabic hybrids might be of great use during work on an etymological dictionary of the Hindi language. It could also be useful for those, who are interested in the linguistic processes taking place nowadays in contemporary Hindi. Hybridisation is not a finished phenomenon. Most of the borrowed formatives are still productive, they interact with the existing lexis as well as with the recent loan-words. Various mechanisms characteristic of Perso-Arabic hybridisation in Hindi are now observed in the huge amount of English borrowings in this language. Word-formatting processes, including hybridisation, are employed for creating neologisms, necessary for developing industry and technology. Hindi-English code-switching and code-mixing has become a common phenomenon in everyday life, in media, in the offices, schools, etc. English-Hindi hybrids of type 1 (compound words) and type 2 (English words with Hindi inflections and formatives) are more and more current, although we still cannot observe the type 3 (Hindi words with English formative components).

The aim, the method and sources.

The main and most important aims of this study are:

1. To show the scale of hybrid Perso-Arabic word-formation in Hindi;
2. To discuss the factors that have been influencing this hybridisation;
3. To point out the features and linguistic processes crucial to it.

The work has been divided into main two parts. The first of them aims to present the whole spectrum of historical, social and linguistic circumstances that have led to this kind of hybridisation. It consists of Chapter I, which comprises the definitions of hybrid given by different authors and describes this feature in the background of contemporary socio-linguistic studies, and Chapter II, depicting historical, linguistic and social factors which have had great influence on Indian syncretism.

The second part includes a linguistic analysis of the collected materials. It starts in Chapter III with presenting the definition of hybrid words, current for this study. Then, in the same chapter, there is a detailed description of all the three above-mentioned types of Perso-Arabic hybrids in Hindi: hybrid compounds (including hybrid compound verbs), hybrids with affixes of Indian origin (including inflexional and derivational forms) and hybrids with affixes of Perso-Arabic origin. Their semantic and statistic characteristics can be found in Conclusion.

In the attached Appendix I a derivational dictionary of Perso-Arabic hybrids in Hindi has been presented. Appendix II comprise a list of cited words and affixes.

The linguistic material for the present study has been collected from *The Hindi-Russian Dictionary* (*Xindi-russkij slovař*), edited in two volumes by V. M. Beskrovnyj in 1972. The dictionary contains about 75 000 words, from among which almost two thousands are Perso-Arabic hybrids (morphological as well as compounds). The choice of this particular dictionary has been brought about by different factors. First, this is the most recent of big dictionaries of the Hindi language. Second, prepared by a group of the best Russian indologists like V. M. Beskrovnyj, A. S. Barxudarov, G. A. Zograf and V. P. Leperovskij, it is at the same time based on excellent Hindi dictionaries[1]. Therefore it seems to be the most reliable source.

All the hybrid words found in the quoted dictionary have been confirmed in at least one of the following dictionaries: Varmā R., *Mānak hindī koś*, vol. 1-5, Platts J., *A Dictionary of Urdu, Classical Hindi and English* and McGregor R. S., *The Oxford Hindi-English Dictionary*. Words of uncertain etymology were additionally checked in dictionaries of the Persian language[2]. Finally, all the collected material was certified by Hindi native-speakers during the author's two-months research staying in India in January-February 2001.

Thereafter the whole selected material has been divided in the three above mentioned groups (types 1-3) and analysed according to the morphological structure of the words. The most

---

[1] These are, above all: Varmā R. *Mānak hindī koś*, vol. 1-5, Prayāg 1968; *Hindī śabdsāgar*, Kāśī, 1926-1930; *Saṁkṣipt hindī śabdsāgar*, Kāśī 1958; *Bṛhat hindī koś*, Banāras 1956; Platts J., *A Dictionary of Urdu, Classical Hindi and English*, London 1884.

[2] Steingass F., *Persian-English Dictionary*, London 1988 (1st ed. 1892); Rubinčik Ju. A., *Persidsko-russkij slovař*, vol. I-II, Moskva 1970.

interesting seems to be the third group – hybrids built by the mean of Persian affixes – for its analysis the comparison with Persian word-formatting processes was necessary.

The last stage of work on the linguistic material was to distinguish and characterise the main semantic groups which – contrary to the previous structural analysis – has been closely connected with the socio-historical background of Hindi-Persian relation.

Transcription.

Roman transcription used in this work differs slightly for Hindi and Persian. As it is usual, the standard Sanskrit transcription with some necessary modifications, has been adopted for Hindi. This type of transcription is used for all the Hindi words cited in this work (including loan-words from Persian); generally speaking, every example preceded with the label H (Hindi) is transcribed according to the following system:

Vowels:

अ *a* आ *ā* इ *i* ई *ī* उ *u* ऊ *ū* ऋ *r̥* ए *e* ऐ *ai* ओ *o* औ *au*

Consonants:

क	*k*	ख	*kh*	ग	*g*	घ	*gh*	ङ	*ṅ*
च	*c*	छ	*ch*	ज	*j*	झ	*jh*	ञ	*ñ*
ट	*ṭ*	ठ	*ṭh*	ड	*ḍ*	ढ	*ḍh*	ण	*ṇ*
त	*t*	थ	*th*	द	*d*	ध	*dh*	न	*n*
प	*p*	फ	*ph*	ब	*b*	भ	*bh*	म	*m*
य	*y*	र	*r*	ल	*l*	व	*v*		
श	*ś*	ष	*ṣ*	स	*s*	ह	*h*		

Modifications denoting characteristic Hindi sounds, absent in Sanskrit:

क़ *k̲* ख़ *k̲h̲* ग़ *g̲* ज़ *z* ड़ *ṛ* ढ़ *ṛh* फ़ *f*

Nasals: anusvāra ं *ṃ* candrabindu ँ *ṁ*

Examples from Persian, which are always preceded with the label P, are transcribed according to standard system of Persian transcription:

ب	*b*	ش	*š*
پ	*p*	ع	^{c}
ت ط	*t*	غ	*ġ*
ث س ص	*s*	ف	*f*
ج	*j*	ق	*q*
چ	*č*	ک	*k*
ه ح	*h*	گ	*g*
خ	*x*	ل	*l*
د	*d*	م	*m*
ذ ز ض ظ	*z*	ن	*n*
ر	*r*	و	*v, ū, o, au*
ژ	*ž*	ی	*y, ī, e, ai*

Abbreviations.

1. Sources and cited literature:

Barxudarov = Barxudarov A. S., *Slovoobrazovanie v xindi*, Moskva 1963.

Beskrovnyj = Beskrovnyj V. M., *Morfologičeskoe gibridnoe slovoobrazovanie v xindi*, [in:] *Xindi i urdu. Voprosy leksikologii i slovoobrazovanija*, ed. Beskrovnyj V. M., Moskva 1960.

BXRS = Beskrovnyj V. M. (ed), *Xindi-russkij slovaŕ*, Moskva 1972.

Čxeidze = Čxeidze T. D., *Imennoe slovoobrazovanie v persidskom jazyke*, Tbilisi 1969.

Dymšic	=	Dymšic Z. M., *Grammatika jazyka xindi*, vol. I-II, Moskva 1986.
Gilchrist	=	Gilchrist J., *A Grammar of the Hindoostanee Language or part 3rd of a System of Hindoostanee Philology*, Calcutta 1796.
Guru	=	Guru K., *Grammatika xindi*, vol. I-II, Moskva 1962.
Katenina	=	Katenina T. E., *Jazyk xindi*, Moskva 1960.
Kellog	=	Kellog S. H., *A Grammar of the Hindi Language*, London 1938.
Lambton	=	Lambton A. K. S., *Persian Grammar*, Cambridge 1960.
Majidi	=	Majidi M. R., *Strukturelle Grammatik des Neupersichen (Fārsi)*, Bd. II *Morphologie*, Hamburg 1990.
McGregor	=	McGregor R. S., *The Oxford Hindi-English Dictionary*, New Delhi 1997.
Pejsikov	=	Pejsikov L. S., *Očerki po slovoobrazovaniju persidskogo jazyka*, Moskva 1973.
Platts	=	Platts J., *Dictionary of Urdū, Classical Hindi and English*, New Delhi 1999.
Rubinčik	=	Rubinčik Ju. A., *Persidsko-russkij slovaŕ*, vol. I-II, Moskva 1970.
Stasik	=	Stasik D. *Język hindi*, Warszawa 1998
Steingass	=	Steingass F., *A Comprehensive Persian-English Dictionary*, Lahore 1981.
Varmā	=	Varmā R., *Mānak hindī koś*, vol. I-V, Prayāg 1968.

2. Other abbreviations:

adj.	=	adjective
adv.	=	adverb
colloq.	=	in colloquial use
dimin.	=	diminutive

esp.	=	especially
f.	=	feminine
fig.	=	figurative(ly)
hist.	=	historical
hon.	=	honorific
m.	=	masculine
med.	=	medical
num.	=	numeral
obl.	=	oblique case
onom.	=	onomatopoeic
pej.	=	pejorative
pl.	=	plural
reg.	=	regional, or local currency
s.	=	singular
tech.	=	technical
transf.	=	in a transferred sense
v.i.	=	verb intransitive
v.t.	=	verb transitive

CHAPTER I

THEORETICAL BACKGROUND

I.1. Hybrid – a definition

The term **hybrid** derives from the Latin word, *hybrida* (< Greek ὕβρις 'wantonness, insolence'), denoting 'offspring of a tame sow and a wild boar, mongrel'[1], and also 'one born of a Roman father and a foreign mother or of a freeman and slave'[2]. Later, for the needs of biological sciences it acquired a wider meaning of:

> Offspring of parents that differ in genetically determined traits [and] may be of different species, genera or (rarely) families. The term 'hybrid', therefore, has a wider application than the terms 'mongrel' or 'crossbreed', which usually refer to animals or plants resulting from a cross between two races, breeds, strains, or varieties of the same species.[3]

From biology and connected fields, the term 'hybrid' has been adopted by some human sciences, such as sociology or linguistics. In recent decades the feature of 'hybridity' has occurred at the very centre of interests of widely ranging social and cultural studies. Hybrids in culture and literature have become subjects for multidirectional analysis, such as in the seminal *Location of culture*[4] or the most recent collection of essays on

---

[1] Klein E., *A comprehensive etymological dictionary of the English language*, Amsterdam 1971, p. 357.

[2] *The Oxford dictionary of English etymology*, ed. Onions C. T., Oxford 1966, p. 454.

[3] *The New Encyclopaedia Britannica*, vol. 6, Chicago 1990, p. 183.

[4] Bhabha H., *The Location of culture*, London-New York 1994.

Indian post-colonial, hybrid literature, edited by Monika Fludernik[5]. In such a sense the term appears also in the Oxford English Dictionary:

> *transf.* and *fig.* Anything derived from heterogeneous sources or composed of different or incongruous elements[6]

The same source points the term's connection with linguistics and defines a term 'hybridism', giving also some examples of its use by different authors:

> In *Philol.* A composite word formed of elements belonging to different languages; *adj.* derived from heterogeneous or incongruous sources; having a mixed character; composed of two diverse elements; mongrel (...).
>
> **Hybridism** *Philol.* The formation of a word from elements belonging to different languages. 'In seamstress and songstress we find instances of *hybridism*' (Latham R. C., *A Dictionary of the English Language*, 1862, p. 480); 'Sometimes we find English and Romance elements compounded. These are termed *hybrids*' (Morris R. *Historical outlines of English accidence*, 1872, p. 39).[7]

Almost identical and similarly brief definitions are offered by a number of dictionaries of linguistics:

> **Hybrid word** – A composed word made up of components which originate from different languages, e.g. *television*, where *tele-* is from Greek *tēle* 'far' and *-vision* is from Latin *visio* 'sight'. Alternative term: **mongrel word**.[8]

---

[5] *Hybridity and Postcolonialism. Twentieth-Century Indian Literature*, ed. Fludernik M., Tübingen 1998.

[6] *The Oxford English Dictionary*, vol. 5, Oxford 1970, p. 480.

[7] *Ibidem*, p. 481.

[8] Hartmann R. R. K, Stork F. C., *Dictionary of Language and Linguistics*, London 1971, p. 105.

Hybrid word – A word composed of elements originating from more than one language (e.g., *automobile*, composed of the Greek *autos* and the Latin *mobilis*). Other name: **mongreal word; Hybrid language** – A language the vocabulary of which contains a great number of borrowed words, terms etc.[9]

Hybrid – A word composed of elements from different languages, for example, *television* comprises elements from both Latin and Greek.[10]

Hybride – En grammaire traditionnelle, un mot *hybride* est un mot composé dont les constituants sont empruntés à des racines des langues différentes. Ainsi, *automobile*, dont les racines sont l'une grecque (*autos*, «de soi-même») et l'autre latine (*mobilis*, «qui peut se mouvoir»), est un *mot hybride*.[11]

It can be easily observed that all the authors understand linguistic hybrids as *compounds of words* of two different origins. Each of these words can exist and function – at least in their source languages – as independent semantic units. Each of these units appears also as a loan-word in many different languages. At the same time, hybrid words composed of them are current in many languages – we have *television* and *automobile* in most European tongues and in every place in the world where these tongues serve as a medium of communication. The explanation of their popularity is quite simple. In Europe it is Latin and Greek that have usually been used for forming new words whenever a need for them appeared. New objects and scientific terms must be named and if they are to be intelligible not only for their

---

[9] Pey M. A., Gaynor F., *A Dictionary of linguistics*, New York 1954, p. 93, 138.

[10] Crystal D., *An Encyclopedic Dictionary of Language & Linguistics*, Oxford 1993, p. 175.

[11] Dubois J. et al., *Dictionnaire de linguistique*, Paris 1973, p. 246.

creators, they must be named with the use of the commonest elements of language(s). On the other hand, the fact that such words as *television* or *automobile* are hybrid has been ordained by chance and their hybridity neither has any particular significance for the speakers, nor for the languages into the system of which they have been accepted as loan-words. They could equally have received a pure Latin or a pure Greek name if the norm were like this.

A different and broader definition of 'hybrid' has been given by R. E. Asher, who describes it as follows:

> **Hybrid combination** – It is a measure of the integration of neo-Classical word-formation items and patterns in general usage in European vernaculars that combinations of neoclassical combinemes with non-Classical items are proliferating, as are native combinations coined on neo-Classical patterns. This is occurring especially, but not only, in trade-names, for example, *agribusiness* or *agrobusiness*, *addressograph*, *resistojet*, *chimpnant*, *Talk-O-Phone*, German *Saftomatic*, *Thermo-Grütze*, *Spielothec*. It has been noted that such combinations, and hence in some cases the combinemes, frequently have a strong connotative value in that they have or are used for a jocular, facetious, or ironic effect, for example, *beerocracy*, *weatherology*; French *mariageomanie*; German *Tretomane*, *Tüteritis*. This effect results primarily from the 'hybrid' combining of items from systems, varieties or registers normally felt to be distinct and separate. Should these systems, etc. be viewed synchronically and functionally rather than etymologically and genetically? Should the hybrids be seen as combinations of learned with popular items, for instance, rather than of native items with those of Greek or Latin origin? Such questions – and they are but two of many – still highlight the need for further study of neo-Classical combinations and combinemes, not least because they can be perceived to hamper intranational communication within a language community or between subgroups of a community, especially between academically trained professionals (scientists, doctors) and lay-

people, even while they may facilitate international communication between (subgroups of) language communities.[12]

Although the main drift of Asher's thought is of no use for our consideration of Perso-Arabic hybrids in Hindi, we still can find in his description an important statement which will appear a basic one while formulating a more traditional definition of the item. This is to look at a hybrid as a combination of the native and foreign elements (contrary to the Greek-Latin examples given by previous authors, which are used everywhere, but nowhere seen as having a 'native' root). The presence of these diverse items leads us to a strong conviction that hybrids appear as an effect of contact between different languages and their speakers. Such a contact is an essential requirement for their creation, and as we will see in the next chapter, the closer and the longer is this inter-language contact, the more such hybrid-words appear.

Another attribute of hybrid-word has been shown in next two definitions:

> **Gibrid** – (gibridnoe slovo, polukal'ka), ang. *hybrid*, fr. *hybride*, nem. *hybrides Wort*, isp. *híbrida*. 'Skreščennoe' slovo, sostavlennoe iz raznojazyčnyx èlementov. Russk. *avtobusnyj*, gde *avto-* < greč. *auto-*, *-bus* < lat. *-bus*, *-nyj* < russk. *n* + *yj*; fr. *bicyclette*. **Gibridizacija** – To že, čto skreščivanie jazykov. **Gibridnyj** – ang. *hybrid* (attr.), fr. *hybride*, nem. *hybride*, isp. *híbrido*. 1) Skreščennyj, smešannyj. **Gibridnyj jazyk** ang. *hybrid language*. To že, čto jazyk smešannyj. 2) Sostavlennyj iz genetičeski raznorodnyx èlementov. *Gibrid-naja forma.* **Gibridnoe slovo**. To že, čto gibrid.[13]

[12] *The Encyclopedia of Language & Linguistics*, ed. Asher R., vol. 9, Oxford 1994, p. 5027-28.

[13] Axmanova O. S., *Slovaŕ lingvističeskix terminov*, Moskva 1966, p. 98.

> **Hybrid word** – One formed from elements that derive historically from different languages: e.g. *amoral*, with a negative prefix (*a-*) from Greek and the rest from Latin.[14]

Here again we have Greek-Latin mixed words, but in both cases the hybridisation is deeper than in compounds of the *television-* or *automobile*-type and concerns derivational formations. The authors of the above-cited examples understand hybrids not only as compounds of two etymologically different words, but also as forms derived from etymologically different stems and affixes. It proves that hybridisation can reach morphology (derivational as well as inflexional[15]) and presumably is the last link in a chain of features caused by contacts between languages.

But to create a full linguistic definition of the term 'hybrid', which will be essential in our further considerations, we have to make a thorough study of the process of its creation, i.e. from the very beginning of the inter-languages contact.

I.2. Hybridisation from the socio-linguistic perspective of India.

In the recent several decades socio-linguistic studies have been developed by linguists of America, Europe and Asia. The observation and description of the results caused by contacts between languages in various circumstances and in different parts of the world has become the main target of these studies. The scholars' attention has been chiefly paid to a scheme, in which an European language (most often English or French) meets local vernaculars used by different Asian or African peoples. Such interests of the Western scholars are surely caused by a long colonial past of Asian and African countries and are probably a result of their "sense of responsibility" for the hybrid

---

[14] Matthews P. H., *Oxford concise dictionary of linguistics*, Oxford 1997, p. 166.

[15] On the inflexional morphological hybrids see p. 76-77.

features that appeared in the post-colonial societies as well as in their languages and cultures.

The case of India, however, is unique, for – what is often stressed – its multiculturalism and syncretism, are not a recent phenomenon. It is well illustrated by the following quotation:

> Hybridity is not a new condition of the postmodern era and is most definitely not a result of British postcoloniality. It is "authentic Indianness" [...] India, divided by many languages and many religious sub-sects, readily gives meaning to the concept of hybridity. The vast number of 'cultures' that give India its diversity blend together to give India its unity and oneness.[16]

However, many statements and theories worked out by contemporary socio-linguists can be useful for research on Indian hybridism, even when focusing on the linguistic processes from several centuries ago. Below I will try to show how the presence and the role of the Persian influences in India could be illustrated in the light of the newest achievements of contemporary socio-linguistics.

Just to start with, we should consider the term **linguistic contact**. According to Hartman and Stork, this is

> the influence of different languages upon each other due to frequent meetings between their speakers. Linguistic contact is characterised by *bilingualizm*, *borrowing*, and *linguistic change*, caused by direct learning, translation and deliberate language teaching. Sometimes mixing of different language forms may create creole or pidgin language.[17]

---

[16] F. Jussawalla, *'Hybridity', Our Ancestral Heritage: Minority 'Indian' Writers Speak of their Diversity*, [in:] *Hybridity and Postcolonialism...*, *op. cit.*, p. 200.

[17] Hartmann R. R. K, Stork F. C., *op. cit.*, p. 51.

A similar definition has been proposed by Crystal:

> **language contact** – a situation of geographical continuity or close social proximity between languages or dialects, so that a degree of bilingualism comes to exist within a community. The languages (also called contact vernaculars) then begin to influence each other, such as by introducing loan words or making changes in pronunciation. The most dramatic examples of new languages arising out of contact situations are pidgins.[18]

It cannot be denied, that both definitions cited above are suitable when characterising the reciprocal relations between Persian and Hindi in the period of their coexistence in India, i.e. from about 12th century (the establishment of Muslim rule in Delhi) to the mid-19th century (the death of the last Mughal emperor, Bahadur Shah, and the actual beginning of British rule), that makes a very long period of about seven centuries. Let us trace now the sequence of features that have been caused by this contact, beginning with the very basic one, which is **borrowing words**. The first definition of linguistic borrowing, given by Sapir in 1921 in his fundamental *Language* says, that borrowing of words is the simplest kind of influence that one language may exert on another[19]. At the same time Sapir points out, that when there is cultural borrowing there is always the likelihood that associated words may be borrowed too and states, that the nature and extent of borrowing depends entirely on the historical facts of cultural relation[20]. On the example of Persian-Hindi this can be well observed – first Persian words appeared in Hindi together with the items designated by them. In the initial period of inter-language contacts, they concerned mostly military organi-

---

[18] Crystal D., *op. cit.*, p. 216.

[19] Sapir E., *Language. An introduction to the study of speech*, New York 1921, p. 193.

[20] *Ibidem*, p. 195.

sation and military rules (cf. *Pṛthvīrāj-rāsau* by Chand Bardāī). Then, in the time of the Mughal rulers, when Persian had become the official language of the Court, both the mass and diversity of Persian loans in Hindi has rapidly increased, embracing military terms, administrative terms, words used in religion, fine arts, poetry, etc. This situation lasted probably up to the first half of the 19th century, when Persian was replaced by Urdu in the function of the official language. It was only a few decades later, in the consequence of escalating nationalistic movements, that both Hindi and Urdu, were finally distinguished to be separate languages[21].

There is no need to repeat here the detailed characteristics of Persian words borrowed by Hindi, done already by some scholars[22]. But one remark, directly connected with the problem of hybridisation in Hindi, is worth remembering here. It can be found in Bahri's book and it denies the opinion expressed by S. K. Chatterji that Persian influence on New Indo-Aryan has been mainly lexical[23]. Bahri, arguing with this statement, says:

> ...although lexical influence is predominant, modern Hindi does contain grammatical and phonological features which can be traced to Persian sources alone [...] Jespersen believes that it is rare for a language to borrow particles, pronouns or verbs [Jespersen O., *Language, its Nature, Development and Origin*, London 1959, p. 211 – A. K.-F.]. The loanwords, according to him, are full words, i.e. words that express complete ideas, viz. substantives and adjectives. But we shall see,

---

[21] Cf. Bahri H., *Persian Influence on Hindi*, Allahabad 1960, p. 17 ff., 111 ff., where the lists of Persian words borrowed in different period and occurring in different Hindi literary works can be found.

[22] E.g.: Tivārī M., *Hindī bhāṣā par fārsī aur angrezī kā prabhāv* [*The influence of Persian and English on the Hindi language*], Vārāṇasī 1969, p. 50-219; Bahri H., *op. cit.*

[23] Chatterji S. K., *Origin and Development of Bengali Language*, Calcutta 1926, p. 117.

> that the Persian loans in Hindi include not only nouns and adjectives, but also prefixes, suffixes, adverbs, conjunctions, interjections and verbs besides fragmentary words, which are quite numerous.[24]

Though Bahri has used the word 'hybridisation', only a few pages further on, he points out that such borrowings, as suffixes, prefixes and fragmentary words, which are the main component of hybrid words, are often excluded by linguists from the loan-words and treated as unimportant 'side effects' of the process of borrowing.

The borrowing of words, especially when on a large scale, entails, of course, some **linguistic changes**. They can concern phonetics, morphology, syntax and even semantics; the more loan-words we can find in the borrowing language, the deeper are the linguistic changes. In the Persian-Hindi case we observe all kinds of them. Their detailed description can be found in the Chapter III.2. of this book.

Another effect of the linguistic contacts is **bilingualism**, or – in some cases – even multilingualism. Following the definition of Meetham and Hudson[25] we find, that most of the types of bilingualism described by them, can be found in India, which from the ancient times has been a multilingual country. So we have here: *diglossia*, a very frequent situation in India, where two or more languages spoken by the same user are varieties of the same language, e.g. literary Hindi and one of its several hundred dialects, that can sometimes be spoken only in one or a few villages; *proper bilingualism* as well as *multilingualism* (according to the number of languages spoken by the same speaker); *native bilingualism*, when there are two mother tongues as well as *non-native bilingualism*, when there is only one 'first' lan-

[24] Bahri H., *op. cit.*, p. 20-21.

[25] Meetham A. R., Hudson R. A., *Encyclopaedia of linguistics, information and control*, Oxford 1969, p. 473-475.

guage and the other one is acquired appreciably later. After the Muslims brought Persian to India and settled their rule over almost the whole country, Indo-Persian bilingualism appeared as its immediate result. Persian was studied by both Hindus and Muslims, if they sought an administrative position. Those who converted in Islam, sent their children to the Islamicised schools, where they mixed their own Indian mother-tongue with the non-Indian tongue of their Muslim colleagues. Both Indian and Muslim writers freely used local speech as well as Persian in their books. In accordance with the definition of Pey and Gaynor, Persian became the **language of colonisation** –

> the language of a politically, economically or culturally superior or strong nation which is imposed upon a conquered or dependent nation or adopted by the latter, as a language of official dealings, business, and as a cultural medium, parallel with or replacing the native language.[26]

Persian in India did not replace native tongues; but – as has been already described – it was used by Indian people, or at least by part of them, as a parallel language. Such interlanguage caused that people who spoke the two languages more or less simultaneously, switched back and forth between them.

> When two languages are spoken by the same individual it is usual for patterns peculiar to one language to be transferred unconsciously into the patterns of the other, (those of the first language normally being taken over into the second), and so to produce divergence from the norm of the second language.[27]

These divergences, commonly referred to as *code-switching*, slowly become a new norm. They concern syntax as well as morphology and in the end may lead to the emerging of a com-

---

26 Pey M. A., Gaynor F., *op. cit.*, p. 119.

27 Meetham A. R., Hudson R. A., *op. cit.*, p. 473.

pletely new form of language. In India the example of such a new form is Urdu. Persian in India never became the language of the masses, but:

> ...it had to intermingle with local languages. The result was Urdu, which is spoken in northern India and is a national language of Pakistan today. A combination of Persian and Hindi, Urdu is a fine example of Indo-Islamic synthesis.[28]

In Urdu Hindi morphology has been combined with a basically local (*tadbhava* and *tatsama*[29]) vocabulary flooded with Persian and Arabic loan-words. The Devanagari script has been replaced by an adapted Arabo-Persian script, although the first often continues to be used[30].

It is very difficult to draw a line between Hindi and Urdu. There are far fewer differences than similarities when we analyse their grammatical system and lexics. In the very first period of their coexistence they were not perceived as distinct languages. In fact in the times of the Great Mughals, in their *darbars* and soldiers' camps, people communicated with each other by means of Hindustani[31], the common north-Indian speech. Of

---

[28] Singhal D. P., *India and World Civilisation*, part II, Calcutta 1993, p. 172.

[29] *Tadbhava* words are words which have evolved organically from Old Indo-Aryan or Middle Indo-Aryan languages; *tatsama* loanwords are words borrowed from Sanskrit, or formed on Sanskrit structural models, which show minimal phonetic adjustment to Hindi phonological patterns (McGregor R. S., *The Oxford Hindi-English Dictionary*, New Delhi 1997, p. xi).

[30] Even today a great stock of Urdu literature is written in the Devanāgarī script. Hindi writers and poets also compose their works in Urdu, but they often can not read Urdu script and they use Devanāgarī.

[31] Some authors, like Zograf or Platts, use the term Hindustani to define Urdu (cf.: Zograf G. A., *Xindustani na rubeže XVIII-XIX vv.*, Moskva 1961, p. 5; Platts J., *A Grammar of the Hindūstānī or Urdū Language*, London 1941, p. 1). Chatterji differentiates two terms:

course, it could differ, according to the region or the social position of the speaker, but still was intelligible for the greater part of the north-Indian society of that time. The actual division into separate languages (Hindi and Urdu) ensued only in the 19th century, as a result of new nationalistic tendencies among Hindus as well as Muslims, skilfully backed up by the British policy of 'divide et impera'[32].

In 1773 John Ferguson, 'captain in the service of the Honourable East India Company', describing the linguistic situation of India, wrote in the preface to his *Hindostan Dictionary*:

> In this extentive continent there are three principal languages: the Sanskrit, the Persish and the Hindostan. The Sanskrit is the language of the Brahmini, preferred by them as sacred from the unhallowed lips or strangers, as the most secret mysteries of their religion. The Persish is confined to the court, to public treaties and negotiations, and to the learned. The Hindostan is the general language of the country, equally understood by all ranks and profession of men, by the learned and ignorant, by the courtier and peasant, and by the Hindoo and Mahomedan: it is therefore the language most useful to a stranger. Besides these three principal languages there are

---

Hindūstānī – a genuinely Persian word to mean the language of Indian Muslims, written in the Persian script and preferring a Perso-Arabic vocabulary (the synonym of Urdu) and *Hindūsthānī* – the Indian form of the same word, which indicates the North-Indian *koiné* (called by him "the great North-Indian *lingua franca*"); cf. Chatterji S. K., *Indo-Aryan and Hindi*, Calcutta 1960, pp. 138-139.

However most of 18th and 19th-century authors used the term "Hindustani" in their grammars and dictionaries describing a common Indian *koiné* (e.g.: J. Fergusson or J. Shakespear – cf. Chapter I.3). Similarly, in the present work I will use the form "Hindustani" to name a North-Indian *koiné*, opposite to "Urdu" denoting a language of Indian Muslims.

[32] Cf. Brass P., *Language, religion and politics in North India*, New York 1974, p. 140-141, 427 ff.

> several provincial ones, such as Bengala, the Urriah, the Telinga, the Malabar, & c. but while each of these is confined within the limits of a particular province, the Hindostan has a much wider range, being understood from the one end of this extensive empire to the other.[33]

Fergusson lists neither Hindi, nor Urdu; he describes the basic 18th-century Indian means of communication, 'the language most useful to a stranger', and calls it Hindostani. In a dictionary published fifty years later (1820), drawn up by John Shakespear, 'oriental professor at the Honorable East-India Company's Military Seminary', we can find another confirmation of the then unity of what is today a diversity:

> The dialect, called zabān-i-urdū, rekhta, hindī or Hindūstānī was formed through the intercourse of the Muhammadan invaders of India with the people they found in that country; and, though its structure is chiefly Indian, yet the materials of which is composed are taken abundantly, almost at pleasure, from the Persian, Arabic, and other foreign languages, as well as from the various dialect peculiar to the Hindūs.[34]

In most of the works dealing with the subject, Hindustani in its form spoken in India before the partition and before its own division into two distinct languages, is usually defined as the north-Indian **lingua franca**[35]. However, when we have a more attentive look at the term itself, we will notice, that it is not fully adequate in this particular case:

> **lingua franca** – in areas of intensive language contact, a language adopted by speakers of different speech communities as

---

[33] Fergusson J., *A Dictionary of the Hindostan Language*, London 1773, 'Preface'.

[34] Shakespear J., *A Dictionary, Hindūstānī and English*, London 1820, 'Preface'.

[35] Cf. e.g. Brass P., *op. cit.*, p. 133, 189, 197; Chatterji S. K., *Indo-Aryan...*, *op. cit.*, p. 138, 212 ff.

> their common medium of communication, e.g. Latin in medieval Europe, Arabic in Near East, Swahili in Central Africa, and Malay in Southeast Asia.[36]

The above definition looks suitable for describing the position of Persian as the mean of communication in the vast territory of Central Asia after the spread of Islam. This Persian, used by Muslim soldiers recruited from various countries and of various mother tongues, this Persian, which to some extent became the usual speech of the common people in their everyday life, this Persian was totally different from the language of classical Persian poetry and literature, from the language of scholars' disputes and even from the language of the Courts. It was a **lingua franca**, *link language*, the supraregional means of communication, of which the aim was to facilitate communication across regional differences[37].

But what about Hindustani then? From the fact that it arose on the basis of one dialect (*Khaṛī Bolī*) we could try to describe it as **koiné**, a specific type of link language, defined by Hock and Joseph as follows:

> …deregionalized languages or dialects which because of their deregionalization become potential vehicles as link languages in areas meeting the above description. The mechanism for deregionalization, in turn, no doubt lies in interlanguage. Koiné […] tends to arise under very special linguistic conditions, characterized by the following features:
>
> – The varieties of speech that are in contact with each other are closely related languages or even mutually intelligible dialects.

[36] Hartmann R. R. K, Stork F. C., *op. cit.*, p. 130.

[37] On *link languages* see: Hock H. H., Joseph B. D., *Language History, Language Change and Language Relationship. An introduction to Historical and Comparative Linguistics*, Berlin-New York 1996, p. 369 ff.

– For cultural or political reasons, these linguistic varieties are considered by their speakers to be of about equal prestige, each being the proper linguistic vehicle for a group with its own cherished identity. Speakers therefore are not willing to give up their speech in favor of one of the other speech varieties.

– No outside language suggests itself as a link language.[38]

All these three conditions are fulfilled in the case of Hindustani. The background of it was one dialect – *Kharī Bolī*, but the others, like Braj or Avadhi, spoken in northern India, which have given their small contribution to the common speech, have been closely related to *Kharī Bolī*. What is more important, Persian, that became the second, after *Kharī Bolī* lexical component of Hindustani, being obviously a separate language, is at the same time its quite close relative, belonging to the same Indo-Iranian group of the Indo-European linguistic family. The next certain thing is that all the dialects/languages used simultaneously in northern India, were of equal importance, although without any doubt, Persian became among them the most prestigious one. However, people did not stop using their mother tongues either in favour of Persian, or of any other language, including Hindustani, and thus bi- or often multilingualism has become in Northern India a very common feature, as they usually spoke the mother language at home but the *koiné* (Hindustani) to communicate with individuals with the mother-tongue different from their own. Another confirmation of the equality of status of the above-mentioned dialects is the fact, that most of them have a rich literary tradition, which in many cases goes back as far as the 14th-15th century.

In the light of the quoted above definitions, the main difference between *lingua franca* and *koiné* could be described as the difference between the level of languages and the level of dia-

[38] Hock H. H., Joseph B. D., *op. cit.*, p. 387-388.

lects. *Lingua franca* is a means of communication for different nations, that use different languages and live in different countries, to which it has been introduced as a strange language, originating outside these countries (it was so in the case of Persian used in many countries and by many different peoples of Central Asia, and among others, in India). *Koiné,* however, is a common speech accepted as the means of communication in different regions of the same country, where people use different dialects (rarely languages) that are closely related to each other, and – what is the most important – it has its source in one of these dialects, and thus it has been originated inside the country where it is spoken. In the case of India the difference is clear, so in the following chapters when referring to Hindustani I will be using the term *koiné*, instead of *lingua franca*, which is the term applied repeatedly by the most authors.

Now we can turn to the phenomenon of hybridisation itself. Its exact analysis has been presented by Keith Whinnom[39], who compared linguistic hybridisation to the same process in biology. Base on the experiences of the latter, Whinnom distinguished between *primary hybridisation* (describing it as a smooth integrating, comparable with linguistic geographical band-frontiers), *secondary hybridisation* (bi- or multilingualism) and *tertiary hybridisation* (leading to the creation of creole and pidgin languages). The first two phenomena we can easily observe in the Indian context – the linguistic contact between Persian and local languages, Indian bi-/multilingualism and their effects on Hindi have been already described above. However, a difference appears, when we come to the Whinnom's third level of linguistic hybridisation. In India tertiary hybridisation neither took the

---

[39] Whinnom K., *Linguistic hybridization and the 'special case' of pidgins and creols*, [in:] *Pidginization and Creolization of Languages. Proceedings of a Conference Held at the University of the West Indies Mona, Jamaica, April 1968*, ed. Hymes D., Cambridge 1971, p. 91-115.

form of creole, nor of a pidgin language. Instead, as a result of this multi-hybridisation (multi-, for more, than two dialects/languages took part in the whole process) two independent languages (Hindi and Urdu) emerged. What is more, these are fully developed languages, possessing their own, separate graphical, phonetical and grammatical systems, and their own vocabularies and literary traditions. But we can still find the third stage of hybridisation in both Hindi and Urdu. This is the hybridisation of the formative system, morphological (inflectional as well as derivational) hybridisation, that occurs in both these languages on a large scale.

Referring again to the biological theory of hybridisation, Whinnom has distinguished four main groups of factors which are necessary for the linguistic hybridisation. These are:

a) factors of contact; they are of seminal importance, for the linguistic hybridisation is not possible without contact. Moreover, the extent, nature and intensity of the hybridisation depend directly on the extent, nature and intensity of the contact. In India the contact between Persian and the local tongues was uninterrupted for about seven hundreds years. It is a very long period, but perhaps even more important is the fact, that there were two parallel social levels, at which this contact had the strongest character. The first was connected with different branches of art, literature, science, religion and philosophy, politics, administration and diplomacy. At this level well-educated people exchanged their languages, supplying the just developing Hindi with Perso-Arabic terms related to the mentioned domains. The second level included various aspects of everyday life, and language used by people in the bazaars, soldiers' camps, etc., and provided Hindi with the great stock of such common words, as the names of cloths, dishes, professions, weapons, and so on. Probably it is just this bi-level contact that has been responsible for the extent and intensity of Perso-Arabic hybridisation in the case of Hindi.

b) factors of attitude; according to Whinnom it concerns the attitude of the speakers of one language to another foreign language, or perhaps even to the speakers of another foreign language. There is no doubt that Persian played in India the role of a prestigious language. Those who spoke it, could get better jobs, were perceived as better educated, as persons of greater culture, members of the elites. But in India the tendency towards giving up the mother-tongues in favour of Persian has never been observed. Perhaps more decisive than an emotional one, at least in the beginning, was the factor of utility. What was borrowed, was that needed, mainly names of items and activities which had not been known before the Muslims arrived to India. However, in the last stage of the reciprocal contact, in connection with the nationalistic movements and purifying tendencies among Hindus and Muslims alike, the factor of attitude became the most important. Nationalists were attempting to clean both Hindi and Urdu of "alien" elements, that were to be replaced by the artificially introduced "own" ones. But even if most of the loan words could be replaced by the already existing or just invented native terms, the morphological hybridisation is practically impossible to remove since many adopted formatives were no longer perceived as "alien".

c) factors of 'outer form'; it can be briefly depicted as the extent of adjusting elements of one language to the phonological (mainly) and grammatical system of the other. The more possibilities exist, the deeper is the process of hybridisation. In other words, the closer are the phonological and grammatical systems of the two languages, the better their elements match each other. In the case of Hindi-Persian the situation seems to be almost ideal. Both languages have originated from the same, Indo-Iranian branch of IE family, both have gone through parallel phases of development, which are characterised by nearly identical linguistic features[40]. When they met in India in 12th-13th century, both tended towards a great simplification, which probably in both cases was caused by the fact, that they were spoken over vast regions, far beyond their primeval territories. Persian, coming from the small, Central Iranian province of Fars, became a Central Asian common mean of communication; *Kharī Bolī*, a dialect spoken in the modest district of Delhi and Meerut, formed Hindustani, the main tongue of Northern India and, later on, of the whole Indian subcontinent. Similar changes simplifying their structure, such as the decline of declension and conjugation, the disappearance of neuter, the strong agglutinative tendency manifesting itself, among other things, in the increasing number of compound verbs, etc., all these caused assimilation of Persian elements to Hindi to be made much easier.

d) factors of 'inner form'; according to Whinnom, it is the mode of perception of reality which is conditioned primarily by the individual's native language, acquired in childhood, conditioned most notably by the semantic and syntactical structure of his language (ideas of hierarchy, contrast, relationship, etc., and of the analysis of events). The barrier that might be caused by this cognitive conditioning forms, Whinnom calls "conceptual". But India and Persia have been neighbours and have had close cultural and trade connections since times immemorial. They exchanged their ideas, customs, personalities, etc., so the way of perceiving reality, these conceptual differences in their case have never been significant. That, of course, has made the task simpler and has enormously facilitated the adapting of new things as well as Perso-Arabic terms, related to them. This great cognitive similarity of Indian and Iranian people can be also proved by the fact, that new words were borrowed even if the needed term

---

[40] Cf. Kuczkiewicz-Fraś A., *Persian elements in contemporary Hindi and their genesis*, [in:] *Zeszyty Naukowe UJ, Prace Językoznawcze* [*Jagiellonian University Linguistic Studies*], ed. S. Stachowski, z. 118, 1997, p. 47-50.

already existed in Hindi. As a result, nowadays we find the Hindi vocabulary full of synonymical words, partly of Indian, and partly of Perso-Arabic origin. They are easily interchangeable, without any alteration in the sense of the whole expression.

When we sum up all the factors described above, we will find the case of Persian and Hindi most favourable for hybridisation. The natural ability of Indian society and Indian culture to syncretise all new features without any own harm and often with great benefit to itself, has played the most important role in this process. Hybridisation that we can find in the language obviously reflects hybridisation in other fields of human activity, from fine arts to the daily duties. Bloomfield stated that "cultural loans show us what one nation has taught another"[41]. Paraphrasing his statement, we can say, that hybridisation shows us which of these lessons has been learned by heart, so, that the new values have been naturalised by the borrowing nation and are no longer felt as "alien".

I.3. Up to date research.

In his article on morphological hybrid word-formation in Hindi, V. M. Beskrovnyj stated:

> Although Arabo-Perso-Hindi morphological hybrids are of great interest from the lexical and grammatical point of view, they have not been investigated as far. In the works dealing with the history of language and studies on grammar, one can find only a very cursory description[42] (transl. A. K.-F.)

The article was published forty years ago (1960), but the quoted opinion is still current. The question of Perso-Arabic hybrids in Hindi has not been described in any comprehensive

---

[41] Bloomfield L., *Language*, Chicago 1984, p. 458.

[42] Beskrovnyj V. M., *Morfologičeskoe gibridnoe slovoobrazovanie v xindi*, [in:] *Xindi i urdu. Voprosy leksikologii i slovoobrazovanija*, ed. Beskrovnyj V. M., Moskva 1960, p. 119.

study. Even the short, 30-page article by Beskrovnyj can be treated only as an attempt at signalling the existence of the problem.

However, when having a closer look at the chapters dealing with Hindi word-formation that can be found in the most books on Hindi grammar – even in those oldest ones – one will come up against some hybrids which have been – knowingly, or not – mentioned by the authors.

Below I will try to summarise what has been written so far about hybrids and the hybridisation in Hindi. For clarity I have divided all the sources into two groups. The first one comprises dictionaries, handbooks and theoretical analysis of Hindi grammar, where usually more or less exhaustive description of Hindi word-formation is included. The second group encompasses works dealing with the influence of the Persian language on Hindi. Finally I will deal with the already mentioned Beskrovnyj's study.

Probably the first book where we can find a chapter dedicated to derivation in Hindi is *A Dictionary of the Hindoostan Language* by John Fergusson to which an outline of Hindustani grammar has been attached. On several pages (54-57) the short description, with examples, of some derivational processes has been given. Among the examples one can trace also a few hybrid words, e.g. *tshokkee* [*cokī*][43] 'ward' – *tshookee-daar* [*cokī-dār*] 'warden'; *bundookh* [*bandūq*] 'musket' – *bundookhee-walla* [*bandūqī-vālā*] 'musketeer'; *jeur* [*jaur*] 'oppression' – *jeur-walla* [*jaur-vālā*] 'oppressor' (p. 55).

The much more exact picture of derivational rules was given by John Gilchrist in his excellent *Grammar of the Hindoostanee Language* published in 1786. The whole chapter VII of this book

[43] In the case of words quoted after different authors, I keep the original spelling, giving at the same time in square brackets their form consistent with international transcription used in this work.

(pages 168-196) entitled "On the derivation and comparison of words" has been composed

> according to the position and nature of the component particles, as Adjunctive, Propositive, Intermidiate or Inflective. And to these, by adding the Arabic Inflections, we shall perhaps include the most of each as properly belong to these [sic!] Chapter; which will moreover be closed with a few practical remarks, on any that do not fall under the above arrangement, and on the compound epithets more strictly so called, with which this, in common with the other oriental languages, abounds.[44]

Gilchrist was the first, who fully knowingly indicated the Persian or 'Hinduwee' origin of the few formatives, pointing, at the same time, if they can be attached to the words of the source different to their own. He gave some examples of such mixed words as well. This is not the proper place for going through the whole chapter although its detailed analysis could be invaluable during research on Hindi etymology. I will again make use of it in the part referred to the linguistic description of hybrid words.

Some hybrids we can find also in the grammars and dictionaries published somewhat later. In *The Dictionary Hindoostani and English* compiled originally by Joseph Taylor, then revised and prepared for print (in 1808) by W. Hunter, for the first time the probable etymology of words has been indicated by putting an initial letter of the name of the source language before the word itself. This method of marking the source language, so obvious for us nowadays, but so modern then, was accepted later by many authors, among others by John Shakespear in his, already cited on p. 30 dictionary published in 1820 and by S. W. Fallon in published in 1879 *New Hindustani-English Dictionary*. So there was A for Arabic, P for Persian, S for Sanskrit and H

---

44 Gilchrist J., *A Grammar of the Hindoostanee Language*, Calcutta 1787, p. 68.

for Hindustani. Sometimes, when the author considered the mixed etymology, he put two letters, like i.e.:

P H *uḥmuqapun* [*ahmak̲pan*] 'folly, stupid' (Hunter)

A H *himmat-vālā* 'high-minded, liberal, brave' (Shakespear) however it does not happen always, as we can see below:

H *gajar* '1. the repetition of the strokes of the gong at 4, 8 and 12 o'clock, and esp. at 4 a.m.; 2. an alarm' but *gajar-dār* adj. 'having an alarm (a clock)' (Fallon), where *gajar* is a Hindi word denoting 'an alarm' and *-dār* is a Persian suffix forming, among other things, possessive adjectives, but the author does not give any indication that the etymology of the word is mixed.

However, the cases when mixed sources were indicated are very rare and the etymology itself is not always sure, which has been pointed out by John Platts in the preface to his outstanding *Dictionary of Urdū, Classical Hindi and English*, published for the first time in 1884:

> Shakespear assigns a word to Sanskrit, or Arabic, etc., simply because he believes (or perceives) that it comes originally from one or other of those languages…[45]

Compiling his own dictionary, Platts made use of the then best existed works on Prakrit, Sanskrit, Persian, Arabic, etc. As he described himself, for many years he has been engaged

> in the study of Urdū and Hindī books (in prose as well as in verse) and newspapers, with the view of collecting words and phrases for this work…[46]

verifying the material collected by previous authors (Shakespear) and supplementing it with "thousands of new words and phrases and additional meanings of words". A lot of space he has set aside for the etymological description of words

[45] Platts J., *Dictionary of Urdū, Classical Hindi and English*, New Delhi 1999, p. IV.

[46] *Ibidem.*

as well as for their derivatives formed by the mean of different affixes. Thus, beside the Hindi-Russian dictionary by Beskrovnyj, which is partly based on it, and the huge, 5-vols. *Mānak Hindī Koś*, the Platts' work, known commonly as "Hindustani Dictionary", has become one of the main sources for this study and most of the hybrid words listed in the Appendix have found their confirmation in it.

Some further examples of hybrid words can be found in *A Grammar of the Urdū or Hindūstānī Language* by G. Small, published in 1895. Although Small does not include any special analysis of derivative processes, he presents a chapter entitled "Denominative and other Derivative Verbs", where he states:

> Very often the original root-word of the verb is either Arabic or Persian, though more commonly an offshoot from Sanskrit or Hindi[47]

and gives some examples, like: *badalnā* 'to change' (from Arabic *badal*) or *ba<u>kh</u>shnā* 'to present, forgive' (from Persian *baxš*).

In the 20th century studies on the Hindi language carried out in Russia (Moscow and Leningrad) yielded several basic books on Hindi grammar and lexicography (sometimes even the term 'Russian school of lexicography' is used). The first of them was a grammatical analysis of Hindustani (Hindi and Urdu) by two eminent Hindi scholars, the Barannikovs[48]. In the chapter about word-formation in Hindi they state that prefixes which in Hindi are usually of Sanskrit or Persian/Arabic origin often join the genuinely Hindi bases, yet they give only one example of such a hybrid word: *bejān* 'dead' (Persian prefix *be-*, meaning 'without'

---

47 Small G., *A Grammar of the Urdū or Hindūstānī Language in its romanized character*, Calcutta 1895.

48 Barannikov A. P., Barannikov P. A., *Xindustani (xindi i urdu). Grammatičeskij očerk*, Moskva 1956.

and Hindi *jān* 'life')[49]. The same combinations can be observed in the case of suffixes:

> ...morphemes of Hindustani origin join both Hindustani and borrowed bases; morphemes of Sanskrit and Persian origin are usually combined with adequately Sanskrit and Persian words, but a few of these morphemes can be also met with words of different than their own source language. [transl. A. K.-F.][50]

and sparse examples are: *yārnī* 'a female friend' < P *yār* 'friend' + H *-nī*, which is a suffix forming fem. nouns; *gāṛībān* 'carter, carrier' < H *gāṛī* 'cart, wagon' + P *-bān*.

T. E. Katenina in her *Jazyk xindi* lists Persian suffixes as a distinct category, next to genuinely Indian (*tadbhava*) affixes and these of Sanskrit origin. But then she describes formatives according to the kind of derivatives they create and a few formatives of Persian origin are included in the *tadbhava* group. Obviously, the author treats these borrowings as being already naturalised in Hindi and equal to Hindi formatives (although Katenina stresses their Persian source). These are following suffixes *-dār*, *-sāz*, *-kār*, *-śāh*, and prefixes: *be-*, *gair-* (of Arabic origin)[51]. Among the examples we can find only few hybrids, like: *naukrānī* 'a servant's wife' < P *naukar* 'servant' + H *-ānī* (forming feminine nouns); *ghaṛīsāz* 'watchmaker' < H *ghaṛī* 'watch' + P *-sāz*; *sāmrājyaśāhī* 'imperialism' < *sāmrājya* 'empire' + P *-šāhī*; *bāzārū* 'of the market-place' < P *bāzār* + H *-ū*. However, Katenina neither uses the word "hybrid", nor pays any attention to the mixed word-formation.

---

[49] *Ibidem*, p. 154. However, the word *bejān* could also have been borrowed as a whole loan, since it exists in Persian, cf.: *jān* 'soul, vital spirit, life' (Steingass 352) and *bījān* 'lifeless; faint; valiant' (Steingass 216)

[50] *Ibidem*, p. 157-158

[51] Katenina T. E., *Jazyk xindi*, Moskva 1960, p. 25-38.

Some Perso-Arabo-Hindi hybrids appear also in Zograf's article on Perso-Arabic elements in Urdu[52]. Although it concerns Urdu, Zograf gives a complete set of Persian and Arabic formatives, many of which function not only in Urdu, but in Hindi as well. He also enumerates some hybrid words among other examples, mentioning the Indian origin of the bases but not paying any special attention to their hybridity. Examples are as follows: *hāthīvān* 'elephant-driver' < H *hāthī* + P *-vān*; *gonddānī* 'a gum-or glue-bottle' < H *gond* 'glue' + P *-dānī*; *pāndān* 'container for betel-leaf' < H *pān* 'betel' + P *-dān*.

In the probably only existing monograph devoted to Hindi word-formation, written by another eminent Russian indologist A. S. Barxudarov[53], we find the chapter on hybrid word-formation. The author counts among hybrids all the words possessing any alien element, different from the genuinely Hindi etymology, and divides them into three main groups: alien words with Hindi affixes; Hindi words with borrowed alien affixes; and words built of two genetically different elements, none of which is Hindi. At the same time he states, that hybrids formed of Perso-Arabic elements (e.g. *k̲arzdār* 'debtor' < A *qarz* 'debt' + P *-dār*), are anymore hybrid feature in the Hindi background and should be treated as homogenous Persian borrowings[54]. On the other hand, Barxudarov sets aside a lot of space for mixed Sanskrit-Hindi and Hindi-Sanskrit words, considering them as equally 'hybrid' as Perso-Arabo-Hindi ones, which – in the light of our definition of hybrid – is a mistake.

Another book by P. A. Barannikov that should be mentioned here is the one about the linguistic situation in the Hindi-

---

[52] Zograf G. A., *Iranskie i arabskie èlementy v urdu*, [in:] *Xindi i urdu. Voprosy leksikologii i slovoobrazovanija*, Moskva 1960, p. 152-245.

[53] Barxudarov A. S., *Slovoobrazovanie w xindi*, Moskva 1963; on hybrid word-formation see p. 90-130.

[54] *Ibidem*, p. 97.

speaking area of India. In this interesting work, describing the main problems of this vast, multi-linguistic region where Hindi plays the role of a predominant language, we also find several pages devoted to Anglo-Indian hybrid word-formation in Hindi[55]. Here, among other features, Barannikov enumerates some suffixes of Persian origin but he does not stress their Iranian source and treats them in common with other, genuinely Hindi affixes, which is quite understandable since Persian formatives were naturalised in Hindi long before English acquired its important position in India. The hybrids cited by Barannikov are: *lāisens-śudā* 'having a licence' < E *licence* + P *-šudā*; *silinḍarnūmā* 'cylindrical' < E *cylinder* + P *-nūmā*; *boṭalband* 'in bottles [milk, etc.] < E *bottle* + P *-band*; *jel<u>kh</u>ānā* 'prison' < E *jail* + P *-xāna*; *beṭikaṭ* 'without a ticket' < P *be-* + E *ticket*.

The last important Russian book worth being mentioned here is a two-volume handbook of Hindi grammar by Z. M. Dymšic. In the preface to the chapter on word-formation[56] Dymšic enumerates hybridisation as one of the main (next to agglutination and calques) methods of developing and enriching a language:

> Hybridisation – forming of new words on the basis of two genetically different elements, e.g.: *dendār* 'a debtor' < H *den* 'debt' + P *-dār*; *bhāṣāvār* 'linguistic' < H *bhāṣā* 'language' + P *-vār* […]; *ġairpārṭī* 'non-party' < A *ġair-* + E *party*. [transl. A. K.-F.][57]

Then Dymšic characterises formatives, one after another, pointing out those of non-Hindi (Persian or Arabic) origin and sometimes (but rarely) it happens that he quotes hybrid-words

---

[55] Barannikov P. A., *Jazykovaja situacija v areale jazyka xindi*, Leningrad 1984, p. 188-202.

[56] Dymšic Z. M., *Grammatika jazyka xindi*, vol. I-II, Moskva 1986; on word-formation see vol. II, p. 83-102

[57] *Ibidem*, p. 83.

among the examples, e.g.: *ṭukaṛkhor* 'parasite, hanger-on' < H *ṭukṛā* 'piece, bit' + P *-xor*; *chatribāz* 'parachutist' < H *chatrī* 'parachute' + P *-bāz*[58].

There are several books where word-formatting processes are described but not a single word has been written about hybrids or hybrid word-formation. Here we can record a two-volume Hindi grammar by Kāmtāprasād Guru, who gives a detailed analysis of formatives used in Hindi (including these of Persian and Arabic origin), but joins them solely to the words of the same origin[59]. Neither R. S. McGregor[60], nor C. Schackle and R. Snell[61], although describing prefixes and suffixes that function in Hindi, mention the feature of hybridity at all.

An attempt at picturing hybridisation in Hindi has been undertaken by Bholānāth Tivārī and Kiraṇ Bālā[62]. In the chapter entitled "Hindī bhāṣā meiṁ saṅkar śabd" [Hybrid words in Hindi][63] they presented some aspects of hybrid word-formation in Hindi, and below I will try to discuss them briefly.

Tivārī and Bālā divide hybrid words in Hindi into five groups, according to the second part of the word. So, successively, we have hybrids with the second part of purely Hindi (*tadbhava*), Persian, Arabic, Sanskrit (*tatsama*) and English origin. Such a way of division creates some strange situations, where, e.g. a word *gairvarg* 'classless' is not treated as a hybrid with a genuinely Arabic prefix *gair-*, but as a hybrid with a sec-

---

[58] *Ibidem*, p. 92.

[59] Guru K., *Grammatika xindi* (transl. from Hindi by Barannikov P. A., Barannikov R. I.), vol. I-II, Moskva 1962; on word-formation see vol. II, p. 179-269.

[60] McGregor R. S., *Outline of Hindi Grammar*, Delhi 1999.

[61] Shackle C., Snell R., *Hindi and Urdu since 1800. A common reader*, London 1990.

[62] Tivārī Bh., Bālā K., *Hindī bhāṣā kī śabd-samracnā* [*Word-structure in Hindī*], New Delhi, no date.

[63] *Ibidem*, p. 165-175.

ond part of Sanskrit etymology (although from the word-formatting point of view in this case the prefix is a distinctive and important part of the derivative).

The authors also included here words which in Hindi can hardly be treated as hybrids: of mixed Hindi-Sanskrit and mixed Perso-Arabic etymology. According to the definition of hybrid word current for this book, this is an obvious mistake. First, Sanskrit elements in Hindi cannot be treated as alien or borrowed in the same sense as Persian or English. Sanskrit is an ancestor of several modern Indian languages and a great part of its vocabulary has entered into the composition of their lexis' in the most natural way of linguistic development. Second, mixed Perso-Arabic words have been brought to India already mixed – we could call them 'hybrids' in the ground of Persian language, where in fact they became mixed. But by India they have been borrowed as a 'ready, finished product' and thus should not be counted among hybrids in Hindi.

Apart from these remarks Tivārī and Bālā made some important statements concerning chronology, the semantic and linguistic value of hybrid words in Hindi; and this part of their book constitutes an important contribution to studies on Indian linguistic hybridisation.

Not too much information about hybrid words in Hindi is included in the books describing Persian influence on Hindi. In the first of them published by Ambikaprasad Vajpeyi we find only the paragraph quoted below:

> We have coined a lot of words in imitation of Persian or Arabic words. These are: *cauparṛbāz* ['a *cauparṛ* player' < H *cauparṛ* 'a game played with dice on a cloth or board of cross-shaped layout' + P *-bāz*], or *pataṅgbāz* ['kite-flyer' < H *pataṅg* 'kite' + P *-bāz*], *samajhdār* ['discerning, intelligent' < H *samajh* 'intelligence, mind' + P *-dār*], *hāthībān* ['elephant-driver' < H *hāthī* + P *-bān*], *bahlbān* ['driver of an ox-cart' < H *bahl* 'a two-wheeled coverd cart pulled by oxen' + P

-bān], *gāṛībān* ['a carter, driver' < H *gāṛī* 'cart, car' + P *-bān*], *modīkhānā* ['a grocer's or merchant's schop' < H *modī* 'a grocer, merchant' + P *-xāna*], *pāndān* ['container for betel-leaf' < H *pān* 'betel' + P *-dān*] and *pīkdān* ['spittoon' < H *pīk* 'juice of chewed betel, spat out' + P *-dān* – all explanations in square brackets – A. K.-F.] (...) A large number of such hybrid words are now used in Hindi, the first part of which is of Persian or Arabic origin and the second of Sanskrit. These are *amrkārak* ['giving orders' < A *amr* 'order, command' + S *-kārak* 'giving, acting'], *zilādhīś* ['district judge' < A *zilā* 'an administrative district' + S *-dhīś*], etc.[64]

Cited already in Chapter I.2. Bahri's book does not contain more particulars on hybrid words in Hindi. It is striking that in Mohanlāl Tivārī's book devoted to Persian and English influence in Hindi[65] (the part concerning Persian influence contains 170 pages) we do not find any mention of hybrid words, although there is a chapter describing Persian formatives borrowed by Hindi (but joined only to Persian or Arabic words – there is no example of a word of mixed etymology). On the other hand, the author has presented several lists of compounds built of the elements of different sources (mainly Hindi and Persian), but he does not use a word 'hybrid' (Hindi *saṅkar*), describing these compounds as 'mixed' (Hindi *miśrit*). Anyway, the work is of great use for those who are interested in the role played by Persian (and English) in Hindi; it is also invaluable when working even on such specialist subject as hybrid words, for it gives many exact particulars about the mechanism of borrowing, adaptations, etc.

There is no doubt that the most valuable text on Perso-Arabic hybridisation in Hindi is still the Beskrovnyj's article cited at the beginning of this chapter. The first important thing about it is that the author describes only morphological features

---

64 Vajpeyi A., *Persian Influence on Hindi*, Calcutta 1935, p. 87.
65 Tivārī M., *op. cit.*

(derivational as well as inflexional), disregarding hybrid compounds. The typology proposed by Beskrovnyj also remains beyond reproach and has become a basis for the typology established in this book. Beskrovnyj has analysed main formatives of Persian and Arabic origin borrowed and used by Hindi, describing how they function in Hindi but without giving any comparison with formative processes current in Persian. The theoretical analysis are supported with numerous examples of hybrid words. In the same manner the analysis of Hindi formatives which join borrowed Perso-Arabic bases has been carried out.

Even though the 30-pages article by Beskrovnyj is the best (and in fact the only proper) work on the subject, yet it lacks some important elements – like the above mentioned comparison between Persian and Hindi word-formatting processes, confirmation of cited examples (only in very few cases a source text is given), a complete – at least to some degree – list of hybrid words or their semantic and statistical analysis. All these defects mean, that Beskrovnyj's text cannot be treated as an exhaustive dissertation on Perso-Arabic hybridisation in Hindi, but rather as an invitation for further research and studies in this field. Present work is an attempt to respond to this invitation.

CHAPTER II

HISTORICAL AND SOCIAL BACKGROUND

II.1. Historical circumstances of Indian syncretism.

A glance at a map of the Indian Ocean shows that the western coast of India was a natural destination for Arab trading dhows from the region of the Persian Gulf. From very ancient times, then, commercial activity had been established and Arabs, long before the advent of Islam, had established a dominant position in the sea trade of several Indian ports. They had their own settlements on the coast, and over the centuries many Arabic and Persian words were in common use in India. This came about, peacefully, as a consequence of trade, and the exchange of ideas between mystics and scholars of both sides. It did not follow any military incursion[1].

Some centuries later Muhammad-bin-Qāsim with Persian soldiers carried out the so-called Arab conquest of India. Muslim travellers in Sindh, in the 8th century, reported that many Arab families were settled there and that this had had some influence on the indigenous language. However it would be too much to expect that there had been any significant influence from Persian, still less from Arabic, on the local language. In fact Muslim settlers benefited from Indian culture and learning, while leaving behind no detectable effect on Indian culture or languages. At that period neither Persia, nor Arabia had anything to compare with India because

---

[1] Cf. Rizvi S. A. A., *The wonder that was India*, vol. II, New Delhi 1995, p. 8 ff.

> Indian attainments in science, literature, arts and culture were really high, and Arabia, or even Persia, till this period, had nothing higher to offer. It had more vigour, but that was physical rather than intellectual. No written literature in Arabic is known to have existed before the Quran. It was during the two centuries of their stay in India that the Arabs really learnt to enrich their literature, especially cultural and scientific. Several Indian astronomers, physicians, philosophers, poets and Pandits are known to have been taken to Arabia to train and help the scholars there in Indian lore. Hundreds of Sanskrit books were translated into Arabic and many others were written under the direction of the Caliphs; but we do not know of any borrowings from Arabic into Sanskrit, Prakrit or later Indian languages. S. Lane-Poole's verdict is definite. He wants us "to dismiss any idea of Arabian influence in India."[2]

Although this nationalistic point of view has as many followers, as opponents, it is unquestionable, that the significant influence began in the 10th and 11th centuries. As a result of the Ghaznavid attacks a large number of people of Turkic, Persian and Afghan descent were brought to India. They were coming to India as soldiers of fortune, as merchant adventures, as scholars and religious men in Islam, as artists and craftsmen. They left their homelands for ever and settled down in the Punjab, around Delhi and possibly in some areas of Gujarat. With the political stabilisation of the Ghori and Slave Dynasties, these strangers started to look on India as their own country, and patronised by the Muslim and sometimes even by the Hindu rulers, they helped to enrich at the same time the medieval culture of India. As S. K. Chatterji states, they brought in a more urban and more cosmopolitan cultural atmosphere, which were much more complex and more sophisticated than the simpler and more primitive culture-world of Hindu India[3]. There followed a slow but steady

---

[2] Bahri H., *op. cit.*, p. 2-3.

[3] Chatterji S. K., *Iranianism*, Calcutta 1972, p. 25.

process of cultural and linguistic integration, "heralding a new era of synthesis of Arab vigour and spirit of inquiry with Iranian graces of life, art, and luxury and Indian love for subjective idealism and genius for achieving unity in diversity"[4]. This process was not all one-sided, a cross fertilisation took place in the field of fine arts, philosophy, and other cultural subjects as is witnessed by, for example, the music and poetic compositions of Amīr Khusrau or the architecture of Qutub Mīnār in Delhi.

At the end of the following century, after the capture of Delhi (1192), the Muslim expanded rapidly into Bengal and as far south as the Deccan. Delhi itself became a centre for divines, poets and scholars. The extent of this immigration from the North and the North-west owed a good deal to the chaos that Chingiz Khan and his Mongols were creating in Muslim countries.

The ruling kings in India made their refugees very welcome. They valued the presence of so much literary talent because of the splendour and prestige with which it adorned their courts. Most of the new arrivals were Persian. They often held key hosts and were among the leaders of the Muslim community in India.

Muslim and Hindu began to live as close neighbours and it is reasonable to suppose each influenced the other. Dress, food, music, art, architecture, and – above all – language, benefited from reciprocal exchanges. It was in North India, i.e. the area of rising Hindi, that most of this occurred. While Muslim scholars studied Hindu philosophy and sciences, such as systems of *Yogā* and *Vedantā*, medicine and astrology, the Hindus began to show more interest in geography, arithmetic, and chemistry – subjects in which the Arabs were making new discoveries.

Some of the Muslim rulers were patrons of Hindu writers a few of whom wrote in Persian; while some Muslim scholars

---

4 *The cultural heritage of India*, vol. V, *Languages and literatures*, ed. Chatterji S. K., Calcutta 1978, p. 643.

wrote in Indian vernaculars. From these exchanges, Hindi veered into a new line which ultimately led to the development of Urdu. Indian Muslims, after the period of permanent struggle, adopted India as their own country and took their wives from among the native women. From this emerged a strong group of people of mixed blood. This was increased by conversions to Islam from the Hindu masses and from a few princely families as well. However numbers told and the immigrant element was gradually absorbed into the overwhelming Hindu majority.

From the 14th century Muslim rulers controlled most of India, except its extreme South and Rajasthan. Following the dissolution of the Delhi Sultanate into a number of regional kingdoms, central authority was soon re-established by the Great Mughals (1526-1707). For our purposes, the Mughal period is taken as starting in 1556 with Akbar's accession to the throne of India, which was followed by India enjoyed a long age of peace and tranquillity. Art and literature, often described as 'syncretic' or 'hybrid'[5], flourished immensely. A mixed Indo-Persian style became a general principle in architecture. Indian elements were commonly used in Mughals' palaces and mosques as well as Muslim arch patterns became popular in Hindu temples and official (or even domestic) buildings. The Persian style of painting brought in by Mughals, inspired both Hindu and Muslims artists and changed on Indian soil into the so-called Mughal school of painting (miniatures). Muslim and Hindu mysticism were by many considered parallel streams which could be made to meet without much difficulty. Classical works of Indian thought were translated and interpreted by Muslim scholars and philosophers for the needs of *sūfī* teachings (e.g. the translation of fifty two Upaniṣads made by Dārā Śukoh or the Islamizing explanation of *Bhagavadgītā* presented by ᶜAbduʾr Rahmān Chisthī). The gen-

[5] Cf. for example Craven R. C., *Indian art.*, London 1991, p. 195 ff.

eral rule characterising this period was tolerance – a common tolerance that enabled both communities to live and develop side by side, and to mix freely at the same time, creating the new, syncretic society.

The long period of Muslim rule prevailed until the 18th century when it yielded to the combination of another invasion from Afghanistan, the internal revolt by the Hindu Marathas, and the ultimately successful expansion of British power. This centuries-long Muslim political dominance naturally had profound effects on the cultural evolution of South Asia, as is perhaps nowhere more evident than in the use of language.

II.2. Arabic and Persian in India.

In the 7th century Islam had spread the use of Arabic as the sacred language of the Quran throughout the far flung lands of the Caliphate. However, as a spoken language it was confined only to the Middle East and North Africa. Further East in Persia and parts of Central Asia, Persian remained the dominant spoken language and soon evolved as a language of literature and administration also. This classical Persian was the most prominent of the Iranian group – a group that is closely related to the Indo-Aryan languages. Even after the spread of Islam and Arabic in the vast territory of Persia, it preserved its Indo-European structure and basic vocabulary, adopting at the same time a huge number of loan-words from Arabic (belonging to the Semitic family of languages quite unrelated to Indo-European) and a slightly modified Arabic script. It was this "Arabicized" Persian that the invaders brought to India as their chief cultural language. As many of their leaders and their troops spoke a form of Turkic as their mother tongue, a certain amount of Turkic elements were also to be found in this Persian. It was known as *fārsī*, from Fars, the Central Iranian province. Its intrinsic simplicity, nouns without gender or cases and an uncomplicated phonemic system, will have helped its spread. In India it was peculiarly acceptable as one of the nearest relatives to the New Indo-Aryan group to which Hindi belongs.

As mentioned above, Persian had been adopted as the literary language of Central Asia. In addition it was the only language that Muslim administrators and noblemen of various nationalities could use among themselves. They had acquired it as a language of necessity. By that time it had been enriched with many Arabic and some Turkic words, while retaining its Aryan structure. In India Persian became a distinctive cocktail of these three elements, and, as such, it was commonly intelligible to most of the foreigners.

Arabic retained a role of some importance. Some knowledge of it was always expected of educated Muslims. Those, who wished to join the clerical establishment had to study it seriously, but it was Persian which was the main medium of Indo-Muslim education. The administration was carried on in Persian. By far the largest amount of royal patronage was devoted to Persian poetry. At the same time, the humble mosque-school (*maktab*) run by the Arabic teachers (*maulavi*) appealed not only to Muslims, but to the many Hindus too, anxious to find a place in the bureaucracy. Some Hindu castes, among which the most important was the Kāyasth, specialised in improving their knowledge of professional skills as scribes and clerks.

As usual in South Asia, few used the same language for writing as for speaking. For many centuries Persian was helped by the steady immigration of native speakers, but they were soon and increasingly outnumbered by local converts. Thus with the fall of Delhi (1192), it was the local Khari Boli (*Khaṛī Bolī*) or 'Upright speech' of the city and its surroundings which – together with considerable number of Persian loan-words – became the foundation of the *koiné* of the Muslim empires which was eventually to give rise to modern Hindi.

While that much is clear, it is not easy to assess how much the language was altered by the Muslim rulers during the 350 years preceding the establishment of Mughal rule in India. The period from the end of the 10th to the middle of the 13th century was not conducive to the growth of literature. Very few literary works of the period are available. A heroic poem *Pṛthvīrāj-rāsau* ("A Poem of Pṛthvīrāj") by Chand Bardāī has traditionally been regarded as the first substantial text written in Hindi[6], as the works prior to it were all in Middle-Indian Prakrits. This particular text contains several foreign (Perso-Arabic) words, which is no longer strange when we consider that its author was a native of Lahore and that the Punjab had already been under the Muslim control for nearly two centuries before he wrote *Pṛthvīrāj-rāsau.* It also describes the war between Pṛthvīrāj and Muhammad Ghori, so we can presume the use of Muslim words was unavoidable. Vajpeyi quotes a verse from the poem which shows, that Chand Bardāī had no reservation about using Persian and Arabic words, and – what's more important – did it with the full consciousness[7]. He also cites a few quotations from *Pṛthvīrāj-rāsau*, underlining words of Persian and Arabic origin and a verse without such elements can hardly be found[8].

The most remarkable person as a scholar, a mystic (*sūfī*) and a poet of these times was Amīr Khusrau (1253?-1325). This son of an immigrant Turk and an Indian Muslim of Turkic descent

---

6 Usually dated as 13th-14th c. Cf.: McGregor R. S., *Hindi literature from its beginning to the nineteenth century*, Wiesbaden 1984, p. 11; Vajpeyi A., *op. cit.*, p. 20.

7 "In giving an idea to the reader as to what this epic poem consist of, he says:

uktidharmaviśālasya rājnauti navaṁ rasaṁ /
ṣaṭbhāṣā purāṇaṁ ca kurānaṁ kathitaṁ mayā // [*samay* 2 *rūpak* 38]

So, the language of the *rāsau* is made up of *ṣaṭbhāṣā* or *ṣaḍbhāṣā*, *purāṇaṁ* and *kurānaṁ*. From *ṣaṭbhāṣā* and *purāṇ* are meant Prakrit and Sanskrit and from *kurān* he means to say Persian and Arabic words" (Vajpeyi A., *op. cit.*, p. 21).

8 *Ibidem*, p. 21-24.

was a fine Persian scholar. He wrote a number of poems and romances in Persian, and he is widely held to be the greatest Persian poet of India. He knew Arabic and Hindi (probably Sanskrit also) – of the last he was especially proud – and was one of the earliest writers of Hindi. However the number of Hindi compositions attributed to him seems to have been modest, consisting only of a few riddles (*paheli*) and bilingual Hindi-Persian couplets (*dohā*). He is also the author of the *K͟hālik͟-bārī*, which is a brief dictionary, in verse, of Persian-Arabic-Hindi synonyms, and students of languages used to get it by heart. This book did a great service in the spread of Perso-Arabic words among the people of North India – as did his other poems, learned by heart and often publicly recited. Thus the language they were written in was coming into use[9].

The Hindi poets who came after Amīr Khusrau used foreign (Arabic, Persian and Turkic) words freely, with the notably exception of Sūrdās, who did so very rarely. However Kabīr, Nānak, Jāyasī, Tulsidās, Bihārīlāl[10], Gaṅg, Bhūṣāṇ and Padmākar had no such inhibitions. There is a marked contrast between Hindu and Muslim poets of Hindi here. Where Hindu made good use of foreign words, Muslim avoided them as far as possible. We find very few of them in the works of Rahīm, Raskhān, Raslīn, Usmān etc.[11] The Muslims also made imaginative use of

---

[9] Cf. *The history and culture of the Indian people*, vol. VI, *The Delhi Sultanate*, ed. Majumdar R. C., Bombay 1970, p. 501-502; Czekalska R., *A Turk of Hindustan*, [in:] *Folia Orientalia. Studia in honorem Stanislai Stachowski dicata*, ed. Chmiel J., Śliwa J., vol. XXXVI, p. 89-96.

[10] The language of *Sattasaī* ascribed to Bihārīlāl (born around 1600), with its frequent Arabic and Persian loan-words "is something new in degree if not in kind and might be called a Hindi antecedent of the literary Urdu of the following century" (McGregor R. S., *Hindi literature...*, *op. cit.*, p. 173-174)

[11] Cf. Vajpeyi A., *op. cit.*, p. 25.

purely Indian themes, although their creative inspiration was derived mainly from a nostalgia for the faded glory of Arabia and Iran. A remarkable example of this feature is the heroic tale of the Rajput Queen Padminī of Chitor that inspired Malik Muhammad Jājasī's *Padmāvatī* written in the 16th century[12].

We have already noted that most of the Mughal Emperors were generous patrons of poets; several were even more, being poets and men of letters themselves. Akbar (reigned 1556-1605), Jahāngīr (r. 1605-1627) and Shāh Jahān (r. 1628-1658) – for a hundred years without a break – extended their patronage both to Persian and Hindi intellectuals. The number of poets that lived and wrote at their Courts was very large – Bīrbal, Ṭodarmal, Mañjhan, Gaṅg, Pukhar, Keśavdās, Sundardās, Cintāmaṇi Trīpaṭhī, Abdurrahim 'Khānkhānā' – to enumerate just a few of them. The same Persian poets often composed their poems in Persian as well as in Hindi. Hindi authors too did likewise. Contact between the two languages and their literary traditions were intimate, and their mutual influences were both significant and inevitable.

Though language of the Court was Persian, everyone could speak Hindi. This situation lasted down to 1837, when Persian was replaced by Urdu. The period between 1500 and 1800 was a golden age of Persian in India.

> It was a time when Persian was, perhaps more zealously studied and known in India than in Persia itself. There have been famous Indian historicians [sic!], translators, philosophers, poets, lexicographers and religious leaders – Hindus and Muslims, who freely and masterfully wrote in Persian. For over two centuries, from the time of Akbar, India led the

[12] The Muslims made a considerable contribution also to other medieval Indian literatures, e.g. Kashmiri, Punjabi or Sindhi (see: *A cultural history of India*, ed. Basham A. L., Delhi 1988, p. 308-309).

world in Persian literature in quality as well as in quantity. Even Persia had a poor show and compared ill with India.[13]

At this time most of the greatest and most powerful magnates and governors liked to employ laureates (rāj kavi) of their own, both Persian and Hindi, who would sing their praises and beguile their idle hours. The Hindi poets went out of their way to include Perso-Arabic words and ideas in their work to make them more intelligible and more acceptable to their paymasters.

Persian was also used very widely in administration and education. All government documents were in Persian. The senior officials of the Mughal administration – both Hindus and Muslims – were transferable throughout the country and wrote their reports in Persian[14]. Apart from its use in administration there were many other causes for the expansion of the influence of Persian. Hindus and Muslims studied together in the same maktabas and madrasas, where Persian partly replaced Arabic taking over the role of the medium of instruction. At Courts and in the harems, the Hindu ladies and Muslim princesses used both languages impartially. Outside in the cantonments, aristocrats, officers and soldiers carried Persian words and practices with them. In the bazaars, shop-keepers were quick to pick up these words to attract and to understand better their customers.

Persian was the language of the ruling class. It was perceived as "better". Its possession conferred a higher status and at least a veneer of culture. In this way it became not only fashionable but a valuable qualification. It was Muslim settlers who

---

[13] Bahri H., *op. cit.*, p. 8.

[14] It was a Hindu, Raja Todar Mal, the Minister of Finance at Akbar's Court, who ordered that all government records had to be kept in Persian (before him records were kept in Hindi). By this simple method he made all officials (including these of Indian origin) learn the Court language of their rulers. See Lane Pole S., *Medieval India*, London 1926, p. 266.

introduced new, that usually meant "more advanced and desirable" sciences, trades, and professions together with new arts and crafts. New words for all these things were needed and they came in as an integral part of the package. They had to be learnt by those, who wished to practice and benefit from these new activities.

All these described above led in the consequence to the most important fact connected with presence of Persian in India: the growth and development of new languages, formed on the basis of the Khari Boli dialect but on a large scale employing Persian vocabulary and script. The most significant of them were Dakhini (*Dakhinī*) and Urdu (*Urdū*).

II.3. The role of Persian in forming new Indian languages.

Dakhini came into existence at the turn of the 14th century in North India and was known in the Delhi Sultanate as *Hindavī* ('Indian'). Towards the end of the 15th century, Dakhini was moved to South India by the armies of Muslim rulers, and it has strengthened there after the Muslim conquest of Deccan. Sometimes Dakhini is described as the form of Urdu used by the Muslims living in South India. Though it came down from Khari Boli, there are many influences of such dialects, as Bangari (*Bāṅgaṛī*), Braj or Bundeli (*Buṅdelī*) in it.

The name 'Dakhini', arisen in the Bahmani Kingdom, signifies 'of South, of Deccan', contrary to 'Hindavi' ('of North'). Though they have a common origin, Dakhini and Hindavi (Urdu) have been developed individually, independently of each other, in different social, economic, ethnic and cultural circumstances. Dakhini acted at first as the current medium of communication between strangers from the North and the local population. What is more, it became, along with Persian, the official language of Courts and literature in Deccan (up to now writings of about 80 authors in Dakhini have survived).

Since the Mughal conquest of the independent Southern duchies in the 17th-18th centuries, literary traditions of Dakhini, supplanted by Urdu, has been declining. To-day, it persists in some form in Andhra Pradesh, Maisur, Maharashtra, Madhya Pradesh, Tamilnadu and Kerala[15]. In Indian tradition, it has been customary to define Dakhini as 'southern Urdu'. But in spite of its Persian script, many Persian and Arabic loan-words and common origin with Urdu, Dakhini is distinguished by a number of separate features in phonology, morphology and spelling (among other things – particular declensions of loan-words, grammatical elements typical of rural jargons in North India – i.e. phrase *mere ko* instead of *mujh ko*, total lack of ergative constructions, so characteristic for all dialects of Western Hindi)[16]. Despite Persian loan-words there are also Sanskrit words in Dakhini. All these things differentiate Dakhini from standard, literary Urdu. Yet, Urdu appeared in South at the beginning of the 18th century, when Dakhini had already started to decay, so, there are no Urdu influences in Dakhini texts[17].

The word Urdu is of Turkic origin and is a short name for *zabān-e-urdū-e mu^{c}alla* ('the language of the soldier's camp'). For the first time the term was used to name a distinct form of language by Khan Arzu (died in 1755)[18]. The long lasting presence and importance of Persian in North India stood in the way of stretching the written form of Urdu – till the beginning of the 18th century it existed only in speech[19]. After the death of Au-

---

15 In accordance with data collected by prof. Masud Husein, in 1974 there were at least ten million people speaking Dakhini in Deccan (cit. after Šamatov A. N., *Klassičeskij dakxini*, Moskva 1974, p. 9).

16 *Ibidem*, p. 8.

17 More on Dakhini can be found in: Šamatov A. N., *Klassičeskij Dakxini*; idem, *Očerki istoričeskoj leksikologii xindi i urdu XV – načala XVIII vv.*, Taškent 1990; Chatterji S. K., *Indo-Aryan..., op. cit.* p. 204-208; Saksena B. R., *Dakhini Hindi*, Prayāg 1952.

18 Bahri H., *op. cit.*, p. 9-10.

19 It is difficult to draw a line between early Hindi and early Urdu. They both had a common stage of development, taking a form of

rangzeb (1707), the last of the Great Mughals, with the decline of the Mughal Court and Persian as the language of its administration and literature, Urdu – supplied by the Deccan poets emigrating to the North – evolved its literary form and has become a full rights cultural language used among Muslims of Bihar, Eastern Uttar Pradesh, Assam, Orissa, Punjab, Bengal, the Maart ha country, Gujarat and Sindh. It adopted the Persian script expanded by the addition of three letters for the specifically Indian sounds (*ṭ*, *ḍ*, *ṛ*) and extracted freely from the Persian (and also Arabic) lexis. Its Perso-Arabic vocabulary and script, as well as its literature (mainly of Islamic inspiration) has become the great recommendations for Urdu among Indian Muslims. But the popularity of Urdu depends directly on the amount of Persian and Arabic vocabulary. Its highly Persianised form, so-called *high-flown Urdū* is unintelligible not only to Hindus (who do not use this language) but also to the large number of Muslims, who are not Persian or Arabic scholars[20].

---

vernacular arisen on the ground of Khari Boli, influenced by the language of Muslim invaders; a North Indian *koiné*, called also Hindusthani (*Hindūsthānī*) (cf.: Chatteji S. K., *Indo-Aryan...*, *op. cit.*, p. 138-139; Grierson G. A., *Linguistic Survey of India*, Patna 1968, p. 42). First signs of differentiation appeared in the 15th century with the beginning of *bhakti* poetry, which was an aspect of reassertion of Indian and Hindu cultural values (including language) against the dominance achieved by Muslim and Islamic elements in North India (McGregor R. S., *Hindi literature...*, *op. cit.*, p. 45).

[20] Cf.: "Urdu in use as the official language of the courts was only slightly different from the Persian it was supposed to have replaced in 1837. The court officers, who were mostly Muslims and Kayasthas, allegedly used a highly Persianised Urdu jargon which was as unintelligible as English to the rural Hindu and Muslim masses alike". Brass P. R., *op. cit.*, p. 131.

CHAPTER III

LINGUISTIC ANALYSIS

III.1. The definition of hybrid in the present study

Summarising all that has been written so far about hybrids and hybridisation, we are able to propose a definition of hybrid, which will be current in this book.

Hybrid in the 'X' language is a word built of two or more elements etymologically different, and complying with all following requirements:

1. At least one of the components must be of alien origin;
2. All the components have come into contact for the first time in the 'X' language;
3. It occurs solely in the 'X' language (then, as a 'finished product', it can be borrowed by other languages).

Let us see what the above definition means in the case of the Hindi language.

By 'native' Hindi elements we understand all these words and formatives (usually Sanskrit) which have been through the processes of historical evolution and therefore differ in form from their etymon (*tadbhava*), as well as words historically derived from Sanskrit, used in Hindi in their unchanged form (*tatsama*)[1]. This assumption eliminates instantly from our study the Sanskrit-Hindi mixed words, which by some authors (e.g. A. S. Barxudarov or Bh. Tivārī and K. Bālā) were treated as regular hybrids in Hindi. In the analysis below all the elements

---

[1] Shackle C., Snell R., *op. cit.*, p. 222.

derived from Sanskrit and used in Hindi are considered as Hindi and marked with the letter 'H'.

Foreign elements in Hindi (so called *videśī*) are mainly borrowed from Persian (and through Persian from Arabic) and English. Much fewer borrowings are from Turkic (at least some of them also by means of Persian), French, Portuguese and Russian. All of them can create hybrid words and hybrid compounds with the Hindi elements, and some of them create hybrids with each other (e.g. *parṭībāzī* 'factional, grouped' < E *party* + P *-bāzī*). Mixed words of the last type are of particular interest. Most of them are built of English bases and Persian affixes. Alien words entering into this type of hybrids have earlier become current in Hindi. Because usually they have also been modified to fit into Hindi phonetic and grammatical systems, we can treat them in this particular case equally to Hindi bases. There are not many of such mixed words but they are also considered as hybrids in Hindi for their components have met for the first time in the Hindi background. Moreover, such words do not occur in other languages than Hindi. Their existence proves the deep naturalisation of the elements of Persian word-formation in Hindi and the great productivity of Persian affixes, as they join loan-words in the same way as genuinely Hindi formatives do.

Since all the Perso-Arabic elements creating hybrid words in Hindi undergo some linguistic changes (which is a natural phenomenon common to every kind of language contact), before passing to the structural analysis of the hybrids themselves, one should do a brief study of adaptations of Perso-Arabic loan-words in Hindi.

III.2. Adaptations of Perso-Arabic loan-words in Hindi. Linguistic changes.

Phonology and script

Phonetic changes, called also sound changes, occur in order to ease in some way the process of pronunciation (here we can find different sorts of simplifications, as assimilation, weakening or loss). Another role of sound changes is to make the mutual communication as successful, as possible and for that purpose some adaptation of the new sounds is unavoidable. It is obvious, that the closer are the sound systems of the two languages in contact, the fewer the number of phonetic changes are observed. In the Persian-Hindi case the main trouble was caused by the fact, that before Persian was brought to India, it had adopted a mass of Arabic words, as well as the Arabic script, which being created for the need of a Semitic language (that Arabic is) is hardly suitable for the requirements of any Indo-Iranian tongue, such as Persian and Hindi. In the consequence, most of the phonetic changes that have occurred in Hindi under the influence of Persian, concern its Arabic elements, and can be found, with some exceptions, mainly in genuinely Arabic words.

The problems with the new sounds that appeared together with loan-words from Persian and Arabic has been resolved in Hindi in three ways.

1. Loss; this has happened to Arabic *ai̯n* (ع) – voiced, pharyngeal fricative that is pronounced by a smart compression of the upper part of the wind-pipe, and the forcible emission of the breath. In the transcription of Arabic and Persian words it is usually signed with ^{c}. In Hindi *ai̯n* disappeared, but vowels after which it stands in Persian and Arabic words, lengthen, e.g.:

P (A) *ba*^{c}*d* → H *bād* 'afterwards'
P (A) *mi*^{c}*da* → H *medā* 'stomach'
P (A) *šu*^{c}*la* → H *śolā* 'a flame, blaze'

2. Assimilation; since the sounds characteristic for Arabic have lost in Persian their distinctive role, they immediately started being pronounced as Persian sounds of close articulation. This way of articulation of Arabic sounds has been then borrowed by Hindi, and their graphical signs have been replaced by adequate Devanāgarī letters.

a) Arabic *ṭā* (ط) which is an emphatic sound and *tā* (ت), in Hindi are pronounced and signed like the voiceless dental plosive H *ta* (त), e.g.: P (A) *ṭabiᶜat* (طبيعة) 'nature, essence, quality' = H *tabīyat* (तबीयत) 'temperament; intrinsic quality';

b) Arabic *ṯā* (ث), *ṣād* (ص) and *sīn* (س), all sound and are written in Hindi alike, as the voiceless alveolar or post-dental fricative H *sa* (स), e.g.: P (A) *xabīṯ* (خبيث) 'impure, wicked, perverse' = H *k͟habīs* (ख़बीस) 'bad, wicked'; P (A) *ṣandūq* (صندوق) 'chest, casket, box' = H *sanduk͟* (संदूक़) 'box; chest, coffer'; P *safed* (سفيد) 'white, fair' = H *safed* (सफ़ेद) 'white, pale'

c) Arabic *ḥā* (ح) and *hā* (ه) are pronounced and written in Hindi like the voiced glottal fricative H *ha* (ह), although in Arabic *ḥā* is voiceless, e.g.: P (A) *ḥāl* (حال) 'state, situation, condition' = H *hāl* (हाल) 'state, condition'; P (A) *himmat* (همة) 'inclination, desire' = H *himmat* (हिम्मत) 'spirit, resolve, courage'.

3. Adaptation of new sounds. Some of alien sounds have been adapted by Hindi in common with foreign words. They occur only in borrowed words and their articulation depends partly on the speaker. It varies from a very exact, proper one, pronounced by some Hindi-speaking Muslims (usually well educated) and linguistic purists, to the form hardly different from adequate Hindi sounds. The assimilation is more common in the spoken than in the written language.

a) Arabic *ḏāl* (ذ), *ḍād* (ض), *ẓā* (ظ) and *zā* (ز) have all one sound in Hindi (as well as in Persian) and are pronounced like the Arabic voiced alveolar or post-dental fricative *za* (ز) being signed with a dotted *j* (ज़). This sound – alien for a genuinely Hindi sound system – occurs in loan-words from Arabic, Persian and English; in the spoken language (rarely in its written form) it tends to be replaced with the Hindi pre-palatal affricate *ja* (ज), e.g.: P (A) *ḏalālat* (ذلالة) 'being abject; baseness' = H *zalālat* (ज़लालत) 'baseness, abjectness'; P (A) *ḍarūr* (ضرور) 'necessary, expedient' = H *zarūr* (ज़रूर) 'certainly, of course'; A-P *naẓar-bāz*

(نظر-باز) 'one who plays with or deceives the eyes' = H *nazarbāz* (नज़रबाज़) 'ts.';

b) Arabic *xā* (خ) which is a voiceless uvular fricative occurs in Hindi only in Persian and Arabic loan-words and tends to be replaced by the H voiceless aspirated plosive *kha* (ख). In Devanāgarī it is transliterated as dotted *kh* (ख़), e.g.: P *baxšīš* (بخشيش) 'a present' = H *bakhśīś* (बख़्शिश) 'a gift, tip';

c) Arabic *ġain* (غ) – the voiced uvular fricative is a voiced correlate of H *kha* (ख) and occurs in the same circumstances. More usually than not it is replaced by the H velar plosive *ga* (ग). In Hindi it is transliterated with dotted *g* (ग़), e.g.: P *maġz* (مغز) brain, marrow' = H *magz* (मग़ज़) 'brain; pitch, pulp, marrow';

d) Arabic *qāf* (ق) – a voiceless, uvular plosive, pronounced similarly to the A *kāf* (ک) and the H *ka* (क), but as far back in the throat, as possible. Similarly to *kha* and *ga*, it occurs in Persian and Arabic loan-words but much more usually than not it is replaced with the H velar plosive *ka* (क). It is transliterated in Hindi as dotted *k* (क़), e.g.: P (A) *qalam* (قلم) 'a pen, reed' = H *kalam* (क़लम) 'a pen; a painter's brush'; P *kināra* (کناره) 'a side, shore, coast' = H *kinārā* (किनारा) 'ts.';

e) Arabic *fā* (ف) – is a voiceless, labio-dental fricative sound that occurs in loan-words from Persian, Arabic and English. As McGregor states, it is articulated "...chiefly in the speech of persons with some acquaintance with Urdu or English"[2]. In Devanāgarī it is transliterated with dotted H *ph* (फ़), e.g.: P (A) *fikr* (فکر) 'thinking; thought, reflection' = H *fikr* (फ़िकर) 'thought; reflection'. In spoken language it tends to be replaced with the H voiceless aspirated plosive *pha* (फ);

f) The Arabic *šīn* (ش) – this voiceless retroflex fricative sound is also a borrowing in Hindi, although the same sound was current in Sanskrit. However, in the Middle Indo-Aryan period

2 McGregor R. S., *Outline...*, *op. cit.*, p. XXII.

the Sanskrit *ṣa* (ष) has changed into the alveolar or post-dental fricative *sa* (स). In contemporary Hindi S *ṣa* (ष) occurs only in genuinely Sanskrit words. The Arabic *šīn* in Persian and Arabic loan-words is usually pronounced like the Hindi voiceless, pre-palatal fricative *śa* (श), e.g.: P (A) *šaiṭān* (شيطان) 'Satan, the devil; a demon' = H *śaitān* (शैतान) 'the devil, Satan; a devil';

g) The Persian voiced dental fricative *že* (ژ) occurs very rarely; in Hindi it is usually confounded with H *za* (ज़) and occasionally changes into H *ja* (ज).

A table given below shows a detailed mutual correlation between Persian and Hindi **<u>consonants</u>** as well as their transliteration in both Persian and Devanāgarī scripts and the standard Latin transcription for Hindi, current also in this study:

PERSIAN	HINDI	TRANSCRIPTION
ک	क	k
ق	क़	<u>k</u>
خ	ख़	<u>kh</u>
گ	ग	g
غ	ग़	<u>g</u>
ś	च	c
ج	ज	j
ژ ز ظ ض ذ	ज़	z
ت ط	त	t
د	द	d
ن	न	n
پ	प	p
ف	फ़	f

ب	ब	b
م	म	m
ی	य	y
ر	र	r
ل	ल	l
و	व	v
ش	श	ś
ث ص س	स	s
ح ه	ह	h

Vowels

The vowels occurring in words borrowed by Hindi from Persian, depict an early New-Persian stage of the development of the Persian vowel system (10th-15th c.). Thus we can observe many differences between borrowed Perso-Arabic words in Hindi and their contemporary Persian forms. This is also the reason, why during the work on these loan-words, the Persian-English dictionary by Steingass is of the greatest use (contrary to other dictionaries, e.g. by Rubinčik, the Steingass' dictionary presents the old stage of vocalisation).

Establishing the chronology of Perso-Arabic loan-words in Hindi is a difficult task because of the lack of written texts – especially from the early period (before the 15th century). The presence of the old system of Persian vowels, however, confirms the hypothesis that most of the borrowings probably came to Hindi before the 16th century, i.e. before its final change into the present form. Probably the study of Perso-Arabic loan-words in Hindi could also have some value for Persian historical linguistics.

Below some examples of such vowel changes are given:

Early New-Persian form (according to the Steingass' dictionary)	A loan-word current in Hindi	A contemporary Persian form (according to the Rubinčik's dictionary)	
P (A) *jăhāz* '..., a ship'	*jahāz* 'a ship, vessel'	*jähaz*	(*ă* → *ä*)
P (A) *bĭsāt* 'sthg. spread out; carpet, bedding'	*bisāt* 'ts.'	*besāt*	(*ĭ* → e)
P *pīr* 'an old man'	*pīr* 'a venerable old man'	*pir*	(*ī* → *i*)
P *pēš* 'before; in front; forward'	*peś* 'ts.'	*piš*	(*ē* → *i*)*
P *muzdūr* 'a mercenary, hired labourer'	*muzdūr* (*mazdūr*) 'a labourer; porter'	*mozdur*	(*u* → *o*)
P *zōr* 'strength, power, vigour'	*zor* 'ts.'	*zur*	(*ō* → *u*)*
P *mūš* 'a mouse'	*mūś* 'a mouse, a rat'	*muš*	(*ū* → *u*)
P *paiġām* 'a message; fame; rumour'	*paigām* 'message; news'	*peyġām*	(*ai* → *ey*)
P (A) *mausim* 'time, season'	*mausam* 'ts.; the weather'	*mousem*	(*au* → *ou*)
P (A) *maujūd* 'found; present'	*maujūd* 'present; at hand'	*mowjud*	(*au* → *ow*)

* Although Steingass does not mark either the length of *ē*, or of *ō*, here they are preserved, just to give a clear view of the whole process.

Morphology

Perso-Arabic loan-words in Hindi become a part of the Hindi grammatical system and a subject to its rules. To make this possible the borrowed words have to undergo some morphological changes.

a) Gender; Hindi, similarly to Arabic, has two genders: masculine and feminine. However there is no direct correlation of gender between Hindi and Arabic because all Arabic loans were transmitted through Persian in which there is no distinction of genders. It can happen that words which in Arabic are feminine, in Hindi take the masculine gender and *vice versa*. The main rule is, that the loan-word takes the same gender as the gender of synonymous words already existing in the borrowing language. Thus, e.g., *kitāb* 'book' which in Arabic is masculine, has changed its gender in Hindi into feminine, analogous to the genuinely Hindi feminine word *pustak* 'book'.

b) Declension; Persian and Arabic loan-words undergo Hindi models of declension by taking Hindi inflections, as can be seen in the exemplifying paradigms given below.

Persian *bačča* (بچه) → H *baccā* 'child, son' (masc.), *baccī* 'daughter' (fem.)

masc.	Direct Case	sg. *bacc-ā*	pl. *bacc-e*
	Oblique Case	sg. *bacc-e*	pl. *bacc-oṁ*
fem.	Direct Case	sg. *bacc-ī*	pl. *bacc-ī*
	Oblique Case	sg. *bacc-ī*	pl. *bacc-iyāṁ*

c) Number; Perso-Arabic borrowings in principal take Hindi plural endings, i.e. masculine nouns and adjectives ending with *-ā* acquire in plural *-e*, e.g.: s. *gūṁgā murgā* 'dumb cock' – pl. *gūṁge murge* 'dumb cocks' (with some exceptions when – similarly to masculine nouns ending with a consonant – they stay unchanged, e.g.: s. *khudā* 'god' – pl. *khudā* 'gods'); feminine nouns ending with *-ī*, *-ā*, have in plural *-āṁ*, e.g.: s. *murgī* 'hen' – pl. *murgiyaṁ* 'hens'; feminine nouns ending with a consonant, have in plural *-eṁ*, e.g.: s. *cīz* 'a thing' – pl. *cīzeṁ* 'things'.

It happens rarely that a loan-word can keep its non-Hindi plural form (it applies usually to Arabic words), although this feature is found much more often in Urdu than in Hindi. Yet, even in Hindi we can find such forms, as *akhbār* '*m.* newspaper' ('broken' pl. of A. *khabar* '*m.* news, information'), *tarafain* '*f.* the two parties (to a dispute)' (dual of A. *taraf* '*f.* side, direction'), *dehāt* '*m.* country, countryside' (pl. of P. *deh* 'a village'), *imārāt* '*f.* building' ('sound' pl. of A. *ᶜimāra(t)* 'building'), etc. However, these words are not perceived as plural forms and act as new words, forming plurals according to Hindi rules, e.g.: s. *akhbār* 'a newspaper' – pl. *akhbār* 'newspapers' (cf.: s. *khabar* 'news, information' – pl. *khabareṁ* 'news, reports'), s. *imārāt* 'a building' – pl. *imārāteṁ* 'buildings'.

Incidentally the Arabic pl. suffix *-āt* or Persian plural suffixes *-hā*, *-ān* can join genuinely Hindi words and create their plural forms, e.g.: *jaṅgalāt* 'woods, forests' < H *jaṅgal* '*m.* jungle, forest'; *karoṛhā* 'tens millions, crors' < H *karoṛ* 'ten million, cror'.

III.3. Perso-Arabic hybrid compounds in Hindi.

In the word-formatting system of Indo-Aryan languages compounds have always played a very important role. In Hindi and Persian this way of enriching the language has been unusually common. In India a detailed classification of Sanskrit compounds has been worked out already by Sanskrit grammarians and the same classification is still used in the grammars of contemporary Indian languages[3].

Hybrid compounds, which in the course of time and as an effect of the growing number of loan-words have appeared in great quantity in Hindi, have become subject to this classification as well. That is why the below presented typology and characteristics of hybrid Perso-Arabic compounds in Hindi refer to this traditional classification.

---

[3] On different types of compound words in Hindi see e.g.: Guru II, 270-300; on hybrid compound words in Hindi cf.: Barxudarov 117-124.

Hybrid compounds, next to the inflexional hybrids (cf. p. 76 ff.), are the simplest kind of hybrid words that can appear in the borrowing language as an effect of the language contact. The only condition, necessary for their occurrence, is a sufficient number of loans that have entered the lexis of the borrowing language.

Perso-Arabic hybrid compounds, as well as other compounds in Hindi, can be divided into the following groups:

a) Collective compounds, corresponding to the Sanskrit *dvandva*, consisting of two equivalent words that would be in the same case and connected by a conjunction if uncompound. The components forming these co-ordinative compounds are usually joined by hyphen, e.g.: *dānā-pānī* 'means of living, (literally) food and drink' < P *dāna* 'grain, seed' + H *pānī* 'water'; *bāṭ-tarāzū* 'weight and scales' < H *bāṭ* 'a weight' + P *tarāzū* 'a balance, scale'.

A particular type of such dual compounds are words the components of which have a different etymology but a synonymous meaning, e.g.: *bāl-bacce* 'children' < H *bāl* 'child; young' + P *bačča* 'child'; *dhan-daulat* 'wealth and riches, accumulated wealth' < H *dhan* 'wealth' + P (A) *daulat* 't.s.'; *moṭā-tāzā* '*adj.* plump, well-fed, sleek' < H *moṭā* 'fat, large' + P *tāzā* 'flourishing, happy'; *pher-badal* 'change, transformation' < H *pher* 'turn, revolution, change' + P (A) *badal* 'change, exchange'.

b) Dependent determinative compounds, corresponding to the Sanskrit *tatpuruṣa*, where one of the members (usually the first one) governs the other (which functions as an attribute of the latter). Most of the compounds are unhyphenated, although exceptions occur, e.g. *khet-mazdūr* 'a rustic, plough-man' < H *khet* 'field' + P *muzdūr* 'workman'; *bīmākartā* 'insurer' < P *bīma* 'insurance, insurance premium or rate' + H *kartā* 'doer, performer, maker'; *peṁśanyāftā* 'having a pension, pensioned' < E *pension* + P *yāfta* 'found, discovered, received, obtained'.

Quite often the former component shows vowel or consonant modification, e.g.: *ghuṛsavārī* 'fancy riding on horseback' < *ghuṛ* (< *ghoṛā*) 'horse' + P *savārī* 'riding, horsemanship';

Usually hyphenated are compounds whose second members are verbal forms, e.g.: *śarārāt-bharā* 'mischievous' < P (A) *šarārat* 'mischievouness, wickedness' + H part. perf. *bharnā* 'to be filled, to fill'.

A separate group of compounds within *tatpuruṣa*-type is made up by **descriptive determinative compounds**, corresponding to the Sanskrit *karmadhāraya*, where the first member, usually an adjective, describes the second, e.g.: *gaṁvārmasal* 'a people's saying' < H *gaṁvār* 'boorish, uneducated' + P (A) *masal* 'saying, proverb'.

The describing component might be also a subjunctive in the function of an adjective, e.g.: *panḍubbī-jahāz* 'submarine' < H *panḍubbā* 'diver' + P *jahāz* 'ship'.

Different type of descriptive compounds is this corresponding to the Sanskrit *dvigu*, in which the first member are numerals, e.g.: *ekrukhā* 'having a single face or side: worked or usable one side only' < H *ek* 'one' + P *rux* 'face'; *ekdarā* 'having a single door; room, hallway' < H *ek* 'one' + P *dar* 'a door, gate'.

c) Possessive compounds corresponding to the Sanskrit *bahuvrihi* – adjectival in nature, referring to a person or thing not denoted by either of the members of the compound. The second member of these is characteristically a noun that loses its character and together with the first member qualifies nouns or pronouns. They are usually unhyphenated. Quite often these compounds have a final adjective suffix, e.g.: *ḍha(k)kan-caśmā* 'protective glasses' < H *ḍhakkan* 'a cover, lid' + P *čašm* 'eye'; *ṭapnāmā* 'a log-book' < H *ṭap* 'hood, roof (of a vehicle)' + P *nāma* 'a writing, a history, book'; *ḍagrāhī* 'wanderer' < H *ḍag* 'a step, or stride' + P *rāh* 'road'; *totāpaṅkhī* 'parrot-winged; golden, bright' < P *tota* 'parrot' + H *paṁkhī* 'wing'; *muṁhzor* 'restive, headstrong, outspoken, foul-mouthed, villainous' < H *muṁh* 'mouth, face' + P *zor* 'strenght, power, vigour'.

d) Hybrid compound nominal verbs[4]. This specific type of compound is common in Hindi as well as in Persian, however the authors of Hindi grammars often skip them[5]. They are formed of two components: nominal part and auxiliary verb. Nominal element means usually a noun or an adjective but in Hindi these can also be participles (functioning in Hindi similarly to adjectives) or adverbs (which according to the traditional Indian grammar are included among adjectives).

The most often occurring verbs forming compounds of this type are *honā* 'to be' (that builds intransitive verbs) and *karnā* 'to do' (forming transitive verbs). Beside these two there are some other auxiliary verbs, like: *denā* 'to give', *rahnā* 'to stay', *rakhnā* 'to put', *lenā* 'to take', *banānā* 'to make', *lagnā* 'to be attached', *lagānā* 'to attach', *paṛnā* 'to fall', *ānā* 'to come', etc.

The nominal part of compound verbs never takes oblique of the plural form, although it plays in the sentence the role of the subject – if an auxiliary verb is intransitive, and a role of the direct object – if an auxiliary verb is transitive.

---

4 McGregor calls them 'conjunct verbs' while the term 'compound verbs' he reserves for composites of verb stems with one of auxiliary verbs; cf.: McGregor R. S., *Outline...*, *op. cit.*, p. 62-65, 80-81, 110 ff., 131-132.

5 Brief descriptions of this type of compound with some examples can be found in: Guru K., *op. cit.*, p. 172-173; Dymšic Z. M., *op. cit.*, vol. II, p. 122-126; Stasik D., *Język hindi*, Warszawa 1998, p. 163-168. Stasik has pointed out an interesting fact that as far as verbs of this type are given by bi-lingual dictionaries, they are usually absent in dictionaries of the Hindi language, cf. for example McGregor's *Oxford Hindi-English Dictionary* or *Xindi-russkij slovaŕ* by Beskrovnyj *versus* Varmā's *Mānak hindī koś*.

Agglutinative tendencies of Hindi have caused compound substantival verbs becoming more and more common. A great part of them are hybrid by nature, since their nominal parts are very often loan-words. Nomina of Persian and Arabic origin are most frequent among these hybrid verbs – in particular Persian participles – although recently the increasing number of nominal components borrowed from English can be also observed.

Hybrid nominal compound verbs in Hindi can employ Perso-Arabic substantives, adjectives (including participles) and adverbs. Examples are given below:

1) verbs composed of Perso-Arabic nouns and Hindi auxiliary verbs, e.g.: *zabān ḍalnā* 'to ask' < P *zabān* 'tongue'; *javāb pānā* 'to be discharged, dismissed' < P (A) *javāb* 'an answer; dismissal, discharge';

2) verbs composed of Perso-Arabic adjectives and participles and Hindi auxiliary verbs, e.g.: *kamzor banānā* 'to weaken' < P *kamzor* 'weak, powerless'; *taiyār karnā* 'to make ready, to prepare' < P *taiyār* 'ready, prepared';

3) verbs composed of Perso-Arabic adverbs and Hindi auxiliary verbs, e.g.:, *peś pānā* 'to surpass' < P *peš* 'forward, in front of'; *der ānā* 'to arrive late (as a train)' < P *der* 'delayed, late'.

III.4. Hybrid words formed by adding Hindi affixes to Perso-Arabic bases (inflexional and morphological hybridisation).

This category (hybrids of type 2) is the next stage in the process of hybridisation. The appearance of this type of hybrid words proves the deep naturalisation of alien loans which are becoming the subject to the native affixation. The necessary condition for this type of word-formatting process is that loans must have already become elements of the vocabulary of the borrowing language. Sometimes such a deep assimilation of a loan-word is confirmed by sound changes or the attaching of inflexional endings characteristic for the borrowing language. In this last case we can speak of **inflexional hybridisation**.

Inflexional hybridisation

In Hindi inflexional hybridisation (called by Beskrovnyj 'morphologisation of loans'[6]) manifests itself in attaching of common Hindi masculine ending *-ā* and feminine ending *-ī* to borrowed Persian and Arabic words. It happens often, that loan-words assimilated this way into Hindi lexis, are becoming subject to Hindi affixation.

A common feature is change of final silent *-h* (ه), transcribed usually as *-a*, and final *-ain* (ع), in Persian and Arabic loans, into masculine Hindi inflexion *-ā* (in plural form this *-ā* changes – as regular Hindi endings – into *-e*), e.g.:

P *parda* (پرده) → H *pardā* 'curtain' (pl. *parde* 'curtains', etc.);

P (A) *fāxta* (فاخته) → H *fā<u>kh</u>tā* 'a (wild) dove, pigeon';

P *čamča* (چمچه) → H *camcā* 'a spoon';

P *dīda* (دیده) → H *dīdā* 'seen; the eye; the sight';

P (A) *naf*^{c} (نفع) → H *nafā* 'profit, gain, advantage';

P (A) *majma*^{c} (مجمع) → H *majmā* 'a place of assembly: an assembly of people'.

A similar change appears in the case of borrowed adjectives, which acquire masculine ending *-ā* that in feminine changes into *-ī*, e.g.:

P *dīvāna* (دیوانه) → H *dīvānā* '*adj. m.* insane, ecstatic' (feminine *dīvānī*);

P *tāza* (تازه) → H *tāzā* 'fresh, flourishing, new' (feminine *tāzī*).

The masculine ending *-ā*, according to the same rules, is sometimes attached also to loans with consonants at the end (nouns as well as adjectives), e.g.:

---

[6] 'Morfologizirovanie zaimstvovannyx osnov', Beskrovnyj V. M., *Morfologičeskoe...*, *op. cit.*, p. 129-131.

P *zaṃbūr* (زنبور) → H *zaṁbūrā* '*m.* a hornet, a large bee; a camel swivel';

P *gung* (گنگ) → H *gūṅgā* '*adj.* & *m.* dumb; one who converses by signs';

P *bīxʷud* (بی‌خود) → H *bekhūdā* '*adj.* unconscious'.

It happens usually in hybrid compounds with second component of Perso-Arabic etymology, e.g.:

P *rāh* (راه) 'way, road' → H *caurāhā* '*m.* cross-roads';

P (A) *manzil* (منزل) 'a house, hotel, lodging' → H *ekmanzilā* '*adj.* single-storeyed'.

Sometimes borrowed Perso-Arabic substantives become in Hindi feminine nouns and attach a feminine ending *-ī*, e.g.:

P *jāmadān* (جامدان) 'wardrobe, cloth-bag' → H *jāmdānī* '*f.* a box, trunk';

P (A) *davāʾ* (دواء) → H *davāī* '*f.* medicine, remedy';

Morphological hybridisation

We can distinguish three groups of Hindi affixes forming hybrids with Perso-Arabic loan-words: a) prefixes; b) suffixes; c) 'half-suffixes'.

a) Prefixes. Prefixation was a common way of forming words in Sanskrit, thus most of the prefixes existing in Hindi are genuinely Sanskrit and appear mostly in words of Sanskrit etymology. Only three from among these prefixes are forming hybrid words with Perso-Arabic loans:

1. ku- 'bad, deficient' (Barxudarov 125; Beskrovnyj 139; Dymšic II 110; Gilchrist 185; Katenina 37; Shackle & Snell 40; Stasik 156).

It forms adjectives of negative quality from nouns, adjectives and verbal forms (participles). While joining substantives, it can also form nouns of the meaning opposing to the basic one, e.g.: *kurāh* 'wrong or improper course' < P *rāh* 'way, road' (Steingass 565).

2. ni- 'out, away, not, without' (Beskrovnyj 139; Dymšic II 110; Gilchrist 185; Guru II 184; Katenina 37; Stasik 154).

It forms adjectives showing lack of the quality contained in the basic word or the quality opposing to one showed by the basic word, e.g.: *nikh̲ālis* 'impure, unclean' < P *xālis* 'pure, unsullied' (Steingass 442).

3. prati- 'each, per, reciprocal, contrary' (Barxudarov 125; Dymšic II 101; Guru II 185; Katenina 37; Shackle & Snell 40; Stasik 156).

It is a very productive prefix, joining substantives and forming nouns and adjectives of the meaning 'opposite to' the basic one, e.g.: *pratisāl* 'each year, every year' < P *sāl* 'a year' (Steingass 642).

b) Suffixes. Suffixation is – next to the composition – the commonest way of forming new words in Hindi. Hindi suffixes which build Perso-Arabic hybrids are as follows:

1. -āī (Barxudarov 103; Dymšic II 96; Guru II 224, 237; Stasik 146).

It forms feminine abstract substantives from adjectival or verbal bases, e.g.: *turśāī* 'sourness, acidity' < P *turš* 'acid, tart, sour' (Steingass 294); *garmāī* 'heat; becoming warm' < P *garm* 'warm, hot' (Steingass 1084); *badlāī* 'exchange, barter; sthg. given in exchange; a replacement; price of exchange' < P (A) *badal* 'change, alteration' (Steingass 164).

2. -ail (Guru II 247)

It is a rarely occurring suffix, joining nouns and forming adjectives. It builds also a few hybrid words, e.g.: *dagail* 'marked, spotted, stained' < P *daġ* 'mark, stigma' (Steingass 528); *gusail*, *gussail* 'quick-tempered' < P (A) *ġussa* '..., anxiety, passion' (Steingass 889).

3. -ānī (Dymšic II 93; Guru II 238; Stasik 147); **-in** (Barxudarov 50, 98; Dymšic II 93, 94; Guru II 22, 240; Stasik 146); **-nī** (Barxudarov 50, 98; Dymšic II 93, 94; Guru II 24; Stasik 147); **-ī** (Dymšic II 93; Guru II 25; Stasik 147).

These four suffixes of great productivity are used for forming female forms of masculine nouns, e.g.: *naukrānī* 'a woman servant' < P *naukar* 'a servant' (Steingass 1435); *darzin* 'a semptress; a tailor's wife' < P *darzī* 'a tailor' (Steingass 512); *fak̲īrnī* 'a female beggar' < P (A) *faqīr* 'possessed of one day's sufficiency for self and family; needy' (Steingass 935); *kabūt(a)rī* 'a hen pigeon; *colloq*. an attractive woman; a village dancing girl' < P *kabūtar* 'a pigeon, dove' (Steingass 1018).

4. -autā (Barxudarov 59; Guru II 229, 248; Dymšic II 91, 96).

This suffix forms abstract nouns from verbal stems and different kinds of nouns as names of receptacles. However, the only known hybrid example is *zamnautā* 'a small percentage paid to one who is surety for some amount' < P *zaman* or *ziman* (that is a corrupt form of *az-man*) 'from me' (Steingass 622).

5. -iyā (Barxudarov 36, 96; Dymšic II 90, 93, 94, 96, 104, 108; Guru II 227, 240; Stasik 147, 149).

This is one of the most productive Hindi suffixes. It joins substantives (nouns as well as substantivised adjectives) and forms:

— nouns of agency (feminine and masculine), e.g.: *k̲ānūniyā* 'a legalistic or litigious person' < P *qānūn* 'a cannon, rule, regulation, law, mode, manner, usage, custom' (Steingass 949);

— feminine diminutive nouns, e.g.: *taṅgiyā* 'ribbon, belt' < P *tang* 'narrow, strait' (Steingass 330); *bagiyā* 'a small garden' < P *bāġ* 'garden' (Steingass 148);

— adjectives, e.g.: *cak̲h̲iyā* 'quarrelsome, ridiculous' < P *čax* '..., war, enmity, opposition' (Steingass 388).

6. -ī (Barxudarov 105-107; Dymšic II 94, 96; Guru II 242; Stasik 147, 149, 150).

One of the most productive suffixes in Hindi as well as in Persian. This fact causes frequent difficulties (sometimes even impossibility) with finding out if a certain word formed by this suffix is a hybrid or not. In Persian this suffix forms adjectives, adjectival substantives and abstract nouns[7]. In Hindi *-ī* plays a double role – it is an inflexional ending of feminine nouns and adjectives (see p. 76) and a word-formatting suffix forming:

— feminine abstract nouns (joining nouns, adjectives and numerals), e.g.: *bidāī* 'dismissal, permission to depart; taking leave; departure; gift given to one departing' < P (A) *vadā*^{c}, *vidā*^{c}[8] 'adieu, farewell; any benediction pronounced on taking leave, parting' (Steingass 1460); *cauhaddī* 'boundary; boundaries of an area' < H *cau-* 'four (in compounds) + P (A) *hadd, had* 'setting bounds; boundary' (Steingass 413);

— masculine nouns of agency (joining nouns), e.g.: *gunāhī* '*m.* a sinner; *f.* sinfulness, guiltiness' < P *gunāh* 'sin, crime, error' (Steingass 1097); *balvāī* '*m.* rioter, rebel' < P *balvā* 'disturbance, disobedience' (Steingass 199); *afīmī* '*m.* opium-eater, opium-addict; *adj.* having to do with opium' < H *afīm* 'opium' < P *afyūn* 'ts.', although the H word *afīmī* might be an adaptation of P *afyūnī* 'an opium-eater' (Steingass 85) and then it cannot be treated as a hybrid word.

— adjectives and adjectival substantives (joining nouns), e.g.: *kasratī* 'taking physical or athletic exercise; developed (the body) by training or exercise' < H *kasrat* 'breaking the body, exercises' (Platts II 833) < P (A) *kasr* 'breaking' (Steingass

---

[7] Cf. Pejsikov L. S., *Očerki po slovoobrazovaniju persidskogo jazyka*, Moskva 1973, p. 76-77, 129-134, 183, 184.

[8] In Hindi the sound *v* is often (especially following consonants and when initial) articulated as bilabial rather, than a labio-dental sound. Thus also in spelling *b* often replaces *v*.

1029); *tandūrī* 'baked in *tandūr* (a kind of clay oven for baking bread)' < H *tandūr* 'an oven' < P *tanūr* 'ts.' (Steingass 331).

An interesting example of morphological suffixation combined with inflexional adaptation is the Hindi word *dārogāī* 'the office or duties of a police inspector or superintendent'. First, a Persian word *dāroġa* (داروغه) 'head man of an office, prefect of a town or village, overseer, or superintendent of any department' has acquired a Hindi masculine ending *-ā* < H *dārogā* '*m.* a police inspector or superintendent' (McGregor 492); then, from such a loan-word, an abstract feminine noun has been created by attaching of Hindi suffix *-ī*, forming in this case a feminine abstract noun (in Persian the same abstract noun has a form *dāroġagī* (داروغگی) 'superintendancy' (Steingass 497)).

Sometimes it is difficult to determine when *-ī* in Hindi plays the role of an inflexional ending of feminine words. It happens usually when the meaning and the category of the Persian loan do not change in Hindi, and the only change concerns the gender of the noun (in Persian it does not have any). Although such loan-words in Hindi are becoming feminine, they do not belong to the above described category of feminine abstract nouns formed by the suffix *-ī*, e.g.: H *zañjīrī* '*f.* chain' < P *zanjīr* 'a chain' (Steingass 642).

7. -īlā (Barxudarov 108; Dymšic II 105; Guru II 244).

It forms qualitative adjectives, which show the possessing of a quality enclosed in the basic substantive, e.g.: *zahrīlā* 'poisonous, venomous' < *zahr* 'poison, venom' (Steingass 630); *barfīlā* 'icy, snowy; snow-covered' < P *barf* 'snow' (Steingass 176).

8. -kaṭ, -kaṭ-ā, -kaṭ-ī (Guru II 209)

It occurs in different words, as: *girahkaṭ* 'a cutpurse, pickpocket' < P *girih* '..., a purse' (Steingass 1085); *dumkaṭā* 'docked, tailed (an animal)' < P *duṃb* (دنب) 'a tail' (Steingass 536).

9. -nā (Barxudarov 46; Dymšic II 118; Guru II 233; Stasik 162).

This suffix forms regular verbs from nominal parts of speech: nouns, adjectives and participles. It can create also hybrid verbs, joining Perso-Arabic loan-words. Among them there are several examples of present stems of Persian verbs, which also function as nominal parts of speech and as such have been borrowed by Hindi, e.g: *guzarnā* 'to pass, to make one's way (past); to elapse, to befall' < P *guzar* 'passing by, pass thou', that is a present stem < P *guzaštan* 'to pass, to pass by' (Steingass 1076); *āzmānā* 'to test, to try, to examine; to try conclusions with (a person)' < P *āzmā* 'skilled, experienced, tried', which is a present stem < P *āzmūdan* 'to try, prove, experiment' (Steingass 44-45).

Hindi hybrid verbs with suffix *-nā* can be also created from borrowed Persian nouns, e.g.: *kharcnā* 'to spend, to use; to bring into use' < P (A) *xarj* 'revenue, tribute, tax, duty' (Steingass 453), adjectives, e.g.: *narmānā* 'to soften; to soothe, to pacify, to assuage; to reduce (as a price), etc.' < P *narm* 'soft to the touch, smooth, sleek, mild, gentle, etc.' (Steingass 1395), adverbs, e.g.: *kamnā* 'to reduce, to decrease, to moderate, to relax, to deduct' < P *kam* 'few, little' (Steingass 1046); *bajānā* 'to perform, to carry out in full, (an order, etc.)' < P *ba-jā* 'in place, true, accurate, right, proper' (Steingass 156).

Hybrid verbs formed this way can be both transitive (as *āzmānā*) as well as intransitive (as *guzarnā*). They can also create causative forms, according to the Hindi verb system, e.g.: *dagnā* 'to be branded (with an iron), to be marked (as with smallpox); to be fired (a firearm)' and *dāgnā* '*I caus.* to burn, *esp.* with an iron, to brand, to mark, to fire (a firearm), etc.' < P *dāġ* 'a mark; scar, spot, freckle, etc.' (Steingass 498).

10. -pan (Barxudarov 102; Dymšic II 97; Guru II 251; Stasik 147).

This is a very productive suffix forming masculine abstract nouns mainly from Persian adjectives, which often have been earlier assimilated to Hindi vocabulary by getting an inflexion *-ā*, e.g.: *gandāpan* 'dirt, pollution' < H *gandā* 'dirty, filthy' < P *ganda* 'fetid, stinking, rotten, filthy, dirty' (Steingass 1099); *gūṅgāpan* 'dumbnes' < H *gūṅgā* 'dumb' < P *gung* 'dumb; one who converses by signs' (Steingass 1100); *dīvānāpan* 'madness, frenzy, mania' < H *dīvānā* 'foolish, insane, mad, furious' < P *dīvāna* 'ts.' (Steingass 555).

11. -ṛā, -ṛī, -rī (Dymšic II 98; Guru II 250, 252).

It forms diminutive substantives, e.g.: *taśtaṛī*, *taśtarī* 'a small plate, saucer' < P *tašt* 'a table bason, a platter' (Steingass 302); *dārūṛā* '*reg.* wine, liquor' < P *dārū* 'a medicine, drug, remedy; a preparation of vinegar and honey, spirituous liquors' (Steingass 497).

12. -tī (Guru II 251).

Its main role is forming deverbal abstract nouns but sporadically it joins also nominal parts of speech, e.g.: *kamtī* '*f.* diminution, scarcity, lack; *adj.* little, few' < P *kam* 'little, few' (Steingass 1046).

13. -ū (Dymšic II 90, 94, 104; Guru II 228, 244).

It forms adjectives from nouns, e.g.: *bāzārū* 'vulgar, coarse (as temperament, speech); crude (in manufacture)' < P *bāzār* 'a market; a market-day; a bargain' (Steingass 144); *dīdārū* 'good to look at, attractive (person) < P *dīdār* 'sight, vision, look; the eye' (Steingass 551).

14. -(ā)vaṭ (Dymšic II 96; Guru II 226; Stasik 146).

This genuinely Hindi suffix creates deverbal nouns denoting the result of an action (described by a verb). There exists one hybrid word with this suffix, formed surprisingly from Persian adjective: *tarāvaṭ* 'dampness, moisture, humidity; coolness, refreshing quality' < P *tar* 'moist, wet, juicy; fresh, green, tender, soft' (Steingass 219)[9].

14. -vālā (Barxudarov 102; Dymšic II 91, 106; Guru II 234, 253; Stasik 148).

This is the most productive Hindi suffix, forming substantives as well as adjectives, declined with gender, case and number, joining nominal and verbal bases. It creates the whole spectrum of nouns and adjectives, as nouns of action, names of professions, possessive adjectives, etc. It is so commonly used that only part of the words formed by attaching this suffix can be found in dictionaries. Examples: *kārkhānevālā* 'factory-owner, industrialist' < H *kārkhānā* 'a factory' < P *kārxāna* 'a shop, workshop, manufactory' (Steingass 1002); *potevālā* 'a treasurer' < H *potā* 'the collected money' < P *pūta* 'a treasury' (Steingass 259); *umrvālā* 'adult, grown up' < *ᶜumr* 'life, life-time, age' (Steingass 866); *nakhāsvālī* 'a prostitute' < P (A) *naxxās* a seller of captives, or cattle taken as plunder' (Steingass 1391); *barābarvālā* 'equal, adjacent, opposite; an equal' < P *bar-ā-bar* 'equal, alike, on a par' (Steingass 167); *śahrvālā* 'a townsman, resident of a particular city or town' < P *šahr* 'a town, a city' (Steingass 769); *śarmvālā* 'shame-faced; bashful, shy; a shame-faced or bashful person' < P *šarm* 'bashfulness, modesty, shame'

---

[9] There exists in Persian (and in Hindi as a loan from Persian – cf. McGregor 441) a similar word *tarāvat* (طراوة) 'being fresh; freshness, moisture' (Steingass 811), borrowed from Arabic, written with initial emphatic *ṭā* and having nothing in common with the Persian word *tar* (تر). But two arguments prove, that a word *tarāvaṭ* occurring in Hindi is a Perso-Hindi hybrid, not an Arabic loan. First, it ends with retroflex *ṭ*, a characteristic Indian sound, which can be found neither in Persian, nor in Arabic. Second, in Arabic script used by Urdu it is written with an initial dental *tā*, not – as in Arabic – with emphatic *ṭā* (cf. Platts 315). Beside all these, a Persian loan-word *tar* 'moist, etc.' is a common word in Hindi, and can be found in most dictionaries of the Hindi language.

(Steingass 742); *tandūrvālā* 'a baker' < H *tandūr* 'an oven' < P *tanūr* 'ts.' (Steingass 331).

c) 'Half-suffixes'. The third type of formatives, occurring in Hindi as well as in Persian, are so-called 'half-suffixes'[10] – words which have their own sense but very rarely appear as independent units. They function as regular suffixes, modifying the meaning of a word they join. There are six 'half-suffixes' creating Perso-Arabic hybrid words in Hindi:

1. -dhārī (Barxudarov 124, 159; Guru II 218).

Genuinely Sanskrit suffix denoting 'wearing, carrying'. There is one example of hybrid with this suffix: *bandūḵdhārī* 'armed, carrying weapon' < P *bundūq* 'a cannon or musket-ball' (Steingass 202).

2. -(ī)karaṇ (Barxudarov 118; Dymšic II 98).

Sanskrit 'half-suffix', denoting 'making, doing'. It functions as English *-isation* and creates abstract nouns, e.g.: *faujīkaraṇ* 'militarisation' < P (A) *fauj* 'troop, squadron; an army' (Steingass 941); *sarkārīkaraṇ* 'nationalisation' < P *sarkār* 'a chief; ..., king's court; government' (Steingass 676).

3. -kṛt (Barxudarov 123).

Sanskrit 'half-suffix', analogous to the previous one, denoting 'made, done', function as English past participle ending *-ed*. Forms adjectives, e.g.: *bīmākṛt* 'insured' < P *bīma* 'insurance, insurance premium or rate' (Rubinčik I 73).

4. -mār (Dymšic II 107).

Denotes 'beating'; forms adjectives and masculine nouns, e.g.: *jamāmār* 'an embezzler, one who escorts money' < P (A) *jam*ᶜ 'collecting, assembling, bringing together' (Steingass 371);

---

10 Russian linguists use a term 'polusuffiksy', which has been employed in this study and translated as 'half-suffixes', and a qualification 'slovosufiksy', that can be translated into English as 'word-suffixes' and in Russian describes this feature much better.

zahrmār 'anti-toxic, antidote' < P *zahr* 'poison, venom' (Steingass 630). It can also attach the suffix *-ī* and create feminine abstract nouns, e.g.: *yārmārī* 'deceiving or cheating, or betraying a friend' < P *yār* 'a friend, lover, companion' (Steingass 1525).

5. -pūrṇ (Barxudarov 122; Dymšic II 107).

Sanskrit 'half-suffix' denoting 'full'; it creates possessive adjectives, joining usually genuine Sanskrit words. The only hybrid word is *jośpūrṇ* 'passionate, ardent' < P *još* 'ebullition, effervescence, agitation (of mind or body); heat, lust' (Steingass 378).

6. -vād(ī) (Barxudarov 118; Stasik 150).

Sanskrit 'half-suffix', denotes 'theory, dispute', creates masculine abstract nouns, e.g.: *naslvād* 'racialism' < P (A) *nasl* 'stock, race, bread, caste, family' (Steingass 1401). Combination of *-vād* and suffix *-ī* forms agent nouns, e.g.: *naslvādī* 'racialist'; *faujīvādī* 'militarist' < P (A) *faujī* '..., troop, squadron; an army' (Steingass 941).

III.5. Hybrid words formed by adding Perso-Arabic affixes to Hindi bases.

Here only these Perso-Arabic formatives are given, which show their productivity in Hindi. That is why affixes moved into Hindi together with borrowed words, as their inherent part, which do not act as elements of Hindi word-formatting system, are not listed below[11]. If an alien affix forms hybrid words, this

[11] D. Stasik, for example, enumerates such Persian formatives as *-ānā* (by the way, its correct Persian form is *-āna* (انه-) – the long *-ā* in Hindi form is only the morphologisation), *-ī*, or *-kār* among other affixes current in Hindi; however, they should not be described as formatives since they have been borrowed by Hindi as parts of loan-words and have never functioned in this language separately. All such loan-words are common in Persian and can be found in Persian dictionaries (e.g.: H *zanānā* < P *zanāna* 'women's apartments, feminine, womanly'

fact proves its productivity on the new ground. It should be stated here, that only these Perso-Arabic affixes can be included into Hindi word-formatting system, which create hybrid words with genuinely Hindi bases.

On the other hand, there are some units, which in Persian are independent nominal parts of speech and members of compound words, but in Hindi they have lost their independence and function only as suffixes (e.g.: *bardār*)[12]. Most of the Hindi scholars define them as 'half-suffixes' or 'word-suffixes' (e.g.: Dymšic, p. 92, 95, 98; Barxudarov, 113-114), similarly to the genuinely Hindi 'half-suffixes' described on page 85-86 (Guru has written that in fact formatives of that type act as members of compounds, but apart from this remark, he enumerates them in common with proper suffixes, cf. Guru, p. 261-264).

a) Prefixes.

1. bad- (Barxudarov 129; Dymšic II 114; Guru 190; Stasik 158).

In Persian *bad* is an adjective meaning 'bad, wicked, naughty' (Steingass 160) and as such becomes a first member of Persian compounds. Authors of books on Persian word-formation do not enumerate *bad-* among prefixes. However, in

---

(Steingass 623); H *dostī* < P *dostī* 'friendship; love, affection' (Steingass 544); H *salāhkār* < P *salāhkār* 'an adviser' (Steingass 791), all were formed on the background of Persian language and were brought to India as "ready products" (cf. Stasik D., *op. cit.*, p. 152).

[12] The main difference between a member of a compound and a suffix is that the latter does not appear in language as a separate unit, with its own semantic and structural value, while the former can act as an independent unit in the sentence. An example is, e.g.: a word **-pasand**, which by several authors is enumerated among suffixes but in Hindi it functions also as an independent word '*adj.* approved, liked; *f.* approval; choice, preference' (McGregor 615) and as such cannot be treated as a suffix, but as a member of compounds.

Hindi (contrary to Urdu) *bad* hardly occurs in a function of an adjective and rather plays the role of a prefix (Barxudarov describes it as a 'word-prefix', similarly to 'word-suffixes') in several old hybrid words, as: *badcalan* '*adj.* ill-behaved; depraved' < H *calan* 'going, moving, proceeding' (McGregor 307); *badḍaul* '*adj.* misshapen' < H *ḍaul* 'shape, form, build, appearance' (McGregor 424).

2. be- (Barxudarov 126; Dymšic II 111; Guru 190; Stasik 158).

In Persian the prefix *be-* (contemporary form *bi-*) is used in scientific terminology and means 'without' (cf.: Čxeidze 10; Majidi 386; Pejsikov 191). To Hindi, as other loan-words, it has been borrowed in its older form *be-* (i.e. before the vocalisation of Persian words has reached its present stage). It is a very productive prefix, forming adjectives depicting the lack of a quality expressed by nouns which it joins, e.g.: *bebas* 'without power, helpless' < H *bas* 'power; command, influence' (McGregor 714); *bedharm* 'unbelieving' < H *dharm* '…, religion; morality; justice' (McGregor 525); *beiñjan* 'without an engine' < E *engine*.

Hybrid adjectives formed by means of *be-* can also attach the feminine suffix of abstract words *-ī*, e.g.: *bebasī* 'powerlessness, helplessness' < H *bas* (see above); *be-dhyānī* 'upset-mindedness' < H *dhyān* 'meditation; reflection; contemplation' (McGregor 535).

3. g̱air- (Barxudarov 126-127; Dymšic II 112; Guru 189; Stasik 157).

In Persian this adjective borrowed from Arabic acts also as a first member of compounds, showing strong tendency towards becoming a prefix meaning '…, other, different; no, not, un-; except, beside, unless' (Steingass 900). In Hindi it functions solely as a prefix, forming substantival and adjectival neologisms, e.g.: *gairlohā* '*m.* non-ferrous metal' < H *lohā* 'iron, steel' (McGregor 903); *gairjānkārī* '*f.* lack of knowledge, or familiarity' < H *jānkārī* 'acquaintance; informed knowledge'; *gairhindībhāṣī* '*adj.* not a Hindi native-speaker' < H *hindī* 'the Hindi language' (McGregor 1071) + H *-bhāṣī* 'speaking; a speaker (of a language) ' (McGregor 766).

Barxudarov cites several hybrid neologisms, built mainly on the basis of Sanskrit and English words current in Hindi and connected with the field of science and politics, but they are mostly unconfirmed by any dictionary of the Hindi language.

5. lā- (Barxudarov 128; Dymšic II 111; Guru 190; Stasik 158).

In Persian this genuinely Arabic (< *lā*) prefix occurs mainly in borrowings from Arabic and means lack of a quality (cf. Pejsikov 193). Similarly, in Hindi the prefix *lā-* 'not; there is not; without' (McGregor 890) can be found mostly in Perso-Arabic loans, with one known exception *lāpatā* '*adj.* lost; wasted; without an address' < H *patā* 'trace, track; information; address' (McGregor 596; McGregor wrongly qualifies *patā* as a Persian word).

4. nā- (Barxudarov 128; Dymšic II 110; Stasik 158).

In Persian *nā-* is a very productive, negative prefix, forming both nouns and adjectives (cf. Majidi 387; Pejsikov 193). In Hindi this prefix, meaning 'not; un-, in-, dis-; without' (McGregor 549) occurs in many Perso-Arabic loan-words, but creates at the same time only a few hybrids, e.g.: *nāsamajh* '*adj.* foolish, unintelligent' < H *samajh* 'understanding, intelligence; mind' (McGregor 984)

b) Suffixes.

1. -(i)cā, **-(i)cī** (Barxudarov 185; Guru II 259).

This suffix, having in contemporary Persian the form *-(i)če* (cf. Pejsikov 179) forms diminutives and as such occurs also in a few words in Hindi. There is one hybrid word – *ḍolcā* '*m.* a bucket', *ḍolcī* 'a small bucket, a small basket' < H *ḍol* 'a bucket or large leather bag' (McGregor 423).

2. -cī (Barxudarov 82).

This genuinely Turkic suffix, forming agent nouns (names of profession) is one of the most productive formatives in Persian (cf.: Pejsikov 179; Čxeidze 29; Lambton 99). In Hindi it has appeared in some Persian loan-words, but joins also a few originally Hindi words, e.g.: *ḍhaṁḍhorcī* '*m.* a public crier' < H *ḍhaṁḍhor(a)* (Beskrovnyj I 675). The best proofs of its productivity in Hindi are hybrid words formed in Hindi by means of this suffix with bases of English origin, e.g.: *golcī* 'goal-keeper' (Beskrovnyj I 481) < E *goal*; *miḍilcī* 'one who has finished a middle school' (Beskrovnyj II 373; Varma IV 357) < E *middle* [*school*].

3. -dān(ī) (Barxudarov 116; Dymšic II 95; Guru II 259; Stasik 152).

The suffix *-dān* in Persian joins nouns and forms names of receptacles (cf.: Pejsikov 180; Čxeidze 29; Lambton 98). In Hindi it plays the same role and creates masculine substantives, e.g.: *ugāldān* 'spittoon' < H *ugāl* 'remains of betel leaf & c. spat out after chewing' (McGregor 114); *cūhādān*, *cūhedān* 'a rat-trap, a mouse-trap' < H *cūhā* 'a rat, a mouse' (McGregor 428); *pāndān* 'a container for betel-leaf' < H *pān* 'leaf; betel-leaf' (McGregor 622); *phūldān* 'a receptacle for flowers' < H *phūl* 'a flower' (McGregor 686). In Hindi this suffix has also a feminine form *-dānī*, created by attaching Hindi feminine inflexion *-ī* and used for forming feminine names of receptacles, e.g.: *dūdhdānī* 'a vessel for milk' < H *dūdh* 'milk' (McGregor 506); *goṁddānī* 'a gum- or glue-bottle' < *goṁd* 'gum, glue' (McGregor 276). Sometimes both suffixes can alternatively join the same base, e.g.: *cūhādān*, *cūhedān*, *cūhedānī* 'a rat-trap, a mouse-trap'.

4. -gar (Barxudarov 112; Dymšic II 90; Guru II 259; Stasik 152).

In Persian this suffix, originated from the Middle-Persian suffix *-kar*, forms nouns of agency and adjectives, joining different bases (cf.: Pejsikov 182; Čxeidze 19-21). In Hindi it appears in a few hybrid names of profession, e.g.: *kāṁsāgar* 'coppersmith' < H *kāṁsā* 'any alloy of copper and tin, or copper and zinc; bell-metal; brass, bronze' (McGregor 185); *gacgar* 'plasterer' < *gac* 'mortar, cement, plaster' (McGregor 250).

5. -gār (Dymšic II 90; Guru II 259; Stasik 152).

In Persian this suffix, originated from the Middle-Persian suffix *-kār*[13], creates nouns of agency (cf.: Pejsikov 182; Čxeidze 20-21). Similarly to *-gar*, *-gār* forms in Hindi a few agent nouns, e.g.: *chāpāgār* 'a cloth-printer' < *chāpā* H 'a stamp, imprint; an instrument for stamping, a wooden stamp' (McGregor 342); *phāṁsīgār* 'strangler, executioner, *hist.* thug' < H *phāṁsī* 'noose, halter, hanging, death by hanging' (McGregor 580).

6. -vān(ī), -bān(ī) (Barxudarov 111; Beskrovnyj 148; Dymšic II 91; Guru II 260).

In Persian this suffix usually occurs in the form *-bān* (cf.: Pejsikov 178; Čxeidze 23; Majidi 391; Lambton 98). The allomorph *-vān* is characteristic for Hindi – *-bān* does not occur in hybrid words in Hindi, we can find this form only in Persian loan-words.

In both Persian and Hindi it joins substantives and forms agent nouns, esp. pointing out the profession or occupation, e.g.: *ūṁṭvān* '*m.* camel-driver' < H *ūṁṭ* 'a camel' (McGregor 136); *bahlvān* 'a driver of an ox-cart' < H *bahl* 'a two-wheeled covered cart pulled by oxen' (McGregor 715). Abstract nouns are formed by the combine suffix *-vānī*, e.g.: *ikkāvānī*, *ekkāvānī* 'f. carriage; transport charges' < *ikkā*, *ekkā* 'a one-horse vehicle' (McGregor 103).

---

[13] The genuinely Hindi suffix *-kār*, developed from Sanskrit *-kār* is, in fact, the same formative as Persian *-gār* and *-kār*. This homophony of Hindi and Persian *-kār* makes it impossible to find out if Hindi nouns formed by means of *-kār* are hybrid or not.

7. -vār (Barxudarov 112; Beskrovnyj 148; Dymšic II 105; Guru II 261; Pejsikov 188; Čxeidze 57-58; Majidi 405).

In Hindi, as well as in Persian, suffix *-vār* forms various adjectives and adverbs, joining substantives, e.g.: *dhārāvār* '*adv.* point after point, orderly' < H *dhārā* 'current; section, article, paragraph' (McGregor 528).

8. -(i)yat (Beskrovnyj 148; Majidi 401).

This genuinely Arabic suffix occurs in Hindi in a few neologisms connected with various fields, as politics, science, etc. It joins substantives, e.g.: *gāndhīyat* 'Gandhism' < H *Gāndhī*; *aṁgreziyat* '*f.* English (or western) ways; cultivation of the English language in India' < Port. *inglês* 'English'.

c) 'Half-suffixes'. This is the most numerous group of borrowed Persian formatives. All but two (-*k͟hānā* and *-śāh*) are deverbal forms of various Persian verbs – most often their present stems – used in Persian extensively in composition and acting as determining components.

1. -band(ī) (Barxudarov 114, 115; Dymšic II 107; Guru II 262).

-Band is a present stem of Persian verb *bastan* 'to bind, shut, close up' (Steingass 186). In Persian it creates nouns of agency and adjectives (cf. Pejsikov 99). In Hindi the 'half-suffix' *-band* has a similar function, joining substantives and creating adjectives and adjectival nouns (masculine as well as feminine), denoting persons possessing an item, which is pointed out by the basic noun, or related somehow to this item, e.g.: *cīrāband* 'one who wears the turban called *cīrā*; also one who makes such turbans' < H *cīrā* 'a turban (of cloth of striped or wavy pattern)' (McGregor 321); *ḍabbāband, ḍibbāband* '*adj.* canned, preserved' < H *ḍabbā* 'a box, carton, container; a tin' (McGregor 418); *ghuṁghrūband* '*f.* a dancer' < *ghuṁghrū* 'a small bell; a

string of small bells worn round the wrist or ankle'[14] (McGregor 289). In Hindi it can also form adverbs, e.g.: *jatheband* '*adv.* formed into group or band' < H *jathā* 'a group, party, band, gang, flock' (McGregor 354).

The compound suffix *-bandī*, in Persian as well as in Hindi, forms nouns of action, names of profession, etc. In Hindi these hybrid substantives are always feminine, e.g.: *ḍabbābandī*, *ḍibbābandī* 'cunning, preserving' < H *ḍabbā* 'a box, carton, container; a tin' (McGregor 418); *khurbandī* 'shoeing (a horse)' < H *khur* 'a hoof' (McGregor 240).

An interesting phenomenon can be observed in both Persian and Hindi, namely, that the suffix *-bandī* functions as an undivided unit, and substantives are created by adding the whole *-bandī* to the base, not *-ī* to the word already suffixed by *-band*. A proof here can be the fact, that both suffixes, *-band* and *-bandī* join freely different bases, i.e. there exist words attaching only *-band* or only *-bandī*, but never both, e.g.: there is in Hindi a word *jālband* '*m.* a carpet decorated with intertwined plants' < H *jāl* 'a net; a network' (McGregor 370), but the word *jālbandī* (?), although grammatically possible and structurally correct (it would have a probable meaning 'decorating a carpet with intertwined flowers'), does not exist. And vice versa, there is a word *phāṭakbandī* 'custody, impoundment' < H *phāṭak* 'gate, entrance; barrier; booth' (McGregor 681), but we will not find a word *phāṭakband* (?) which – if it existed – could probably mean 'arrested; one being looked after'.

2. -bardār(ī) (Guru 263)

This is an interesting example of Persian nominal part of speech that has changed into a suffix in Hindi. The word *bardār* in Persian is a present stem of the compound verb *bar-dāštan* 'to exalt, raise, elevate, to bear up, support, pick up, etc.' And as a

[14] Such strings of bells are always worn by dancers during the performance.

member of compounds has a meaning 'bearing, supporting, raising, or holding up", although it functions also as an independent word (Steingass 172). In Hindi it appeared as a part of borrowed Persian compouned words (as, e.g.: *hukkābardār* 'servant responsible for a hookah') and after some time it has started acting as a suffix, losing its independence (in Hindi the independent word *bardār* does not occur). Suffix *-bardār* in Hindi means 'bearing, bearer' and joining nouns, it forms masculine names of profession or occupation, e.g.: *jhāṛūbardār* 'a sweeper' < H *jhāṛū* 'a broom' (McGregor 393); *cilambardār* 'one who prepares a *cilam* (pipe) or a hookah (water-pipe)' < H *cilam* 'a clay bowl with or without stem, in which tobacco, & c. is smoked' (McGregor 320).

Nouns formed by the mean of *-bardār* can join Hindi suffix *-ī* and build names of action, as *thailībardārī* '*f.* carrying sacks, bags; a tax for carrying bags' < H *thailībardār* 'one who carries bags, sacks, from place to place' < *thailī* 'a bag, a sack' (McGregor 471).

3. -bāz(ī) (Barxudarov 113; Dymšic II 92, 107; Guru II 263; Stasik 153).

In Persian *bāz* is a present stem of the verb *bāxtan* 'to play' and as a member of compounds means 'playing at, with, or on, staking' (Steingass 143). In Hindi, as other similar loans, it has changed its category, becoming a noun formant creating various adjectives and masculine (with a few exceptions) nouns, e.g.: *gapoṛebāz* '*m.* gossip; scandalmonger' < H *gapoṛā* 'baseless or exaggerated remark; rumour' (McGregor, 254); *ghūṁsebāz* '*m.* a boxer' < H *ghūṁsā* 'a blow with the fist; a fist' (McGregor 291); *cālbāz* '*adj.* deceitful, fraudulent; *m.* a deceitful person' < H *cāl* 'practice, custom, fashion, procedure' (McGregor 312); *cuhalbāz* '*adj.* merry, light-hearted, amusing, naughty' < H *cuhal* 'merriment; naughtiness (of behaviour)' (Mc Gregor 326); *dhagaṛbāz* '*f.* an adultress' < H *dhagaṛ*, *dhagṛā* 'lover, adulterer' (McGregor 520).

The suffix *-bāzī* is, in fact, composed of P *-bāz* and Hindi suffix *-ī*, forming feminine abstract nouns and – similarly to *-band / -bandī* – both of them can join various bases independently, e.g.: *kalābāz* '*m.* an acrobat', *kalābāzī* '*f.* acrobatics, somersault' < *kalā* 'an art; a skill or accomplishment; trick, juggling' (McGregor 178); *kaukauvebāzī* '*f.* flying kites' < H *kaukauvā* 'a large, square, paper kite' (McGregor 164), but there is no word *kaukauvebāz* (?) in Hindi. It can join also English bases, e.g.: *posṭarbāzī* 'advertising, plackarding' < E *poster*. Both *-bāz* and *-bāzī* are very productive Hindi formatives.

4. -dār(ī) (Barxudarov 97-99, 111; Dymšic II 91, 105; Guru II 262; Stasik 153).

In Persian *-dār* is a present stem of the verb *dāštan* 'to have, to hold, to possess' and occurs as a member of compounds, meaning 'holding, possessing, keeping; a keeper, possessor, lord' (Steingass 495). In Persian *-dār* is a very productive unit and some scholars count it among suffixes, similarly as *-bān / -vān* (cf. Čxeidze, p. 104-105 and footnote 3, p. 104)[15].

In Hindi *-dār* turns out to be one of the most productive suffixes of the whole system, and one that is most often used from among all Perso-Arabic formatives borrowed by Hindi. It forms possessive adjectives and nouns, acting similarly to a genuinely Hindi suffix *-vālā*, i.e. joining singular and plural nouns in the oblique form, e.g.: *kāṁṭedār* '*adj.* thorny, barbed' < H *kāṁṭā* 'thorn; sting' (McGregor 185); *caktiyoṁdār* '*adj.* patched (clothes)' < H *caktiyoṁ* = obl. pl. of H *caktī* '*f.* a round or squarish piece (as of cloth, leather, metal); a patch' (McGregor

---

[15] McGregor defines similarly the function of *-dār* in Hindi: "-dār [P: present stem of *dāštan*] adj. & m. in comp., esp. as second member forming adjectives and nouns. having, holding; possessor, &c...." (McGregor 492), however, since in Hindi it has lost its independence and semantic value, not occurring separately in a sentence, it cannot be defined as a member of compound but as a suffix.

296); *royendār* '*adj*. hairy, woolly, furred' < *royeṁ* = obl. pl. of H *royaṁ* '*m*. body hair; animal hair; wool; fur' (McGregor 873)[16]. Adjectives formed by means of *-dār* are of great variety and can describe different kinds of items and beings, e.g.: *aṛdār* 'stubborn' < H *aṛ* 'obstinacy, contention, dispute' (McGregor 20); *uljhandār* 'tangled, intricate' < H *uljhan* 'tangled state, tangle' (McGregor 132); *khanakdār* '*onom.* ringing, clinking, jingling' < H *khanak* 'a ringing, clinking, or jingling sound; a clashing or clanking sound; clattering' (McGregor 228); *cheddār* 'full of holes' < H *ched* 'a hole; an opening, gap, crack' (McGregor 348); *ṭopīdār* 'wearing a hat' < H *ṭopī* a hat, cap, hood' (McGregor 407); *dābdār* 'powerful, mighty, awesome, oppressive' < H *dāb* 'pressure, weight; power, authority, control' (McGregor 490); *ḍaṅkdār* 'having a sting' < H *ḍaṅk* 'a sting' (McGregor 416).

Substantives formed by suffix *-dār* (always masculine) are nouns of agency, usually describing kind of profession or occupation carrying out by a person, e.g.: *āṛhatdār* 'agent, broker, stock-broker' < H *āṛhat* 'an agency, brokerage, business; warehouse' (McGregor 83); *cakledār* 'the administrator and collector of revenues of a *caklā* (brothel) < H *caklā* 'brothel' (McGregor 296); *palledār* 'a porter' < H *pallā* 'a sack for grain; a burden' (McGregor 613; *pūṁjīdār* 'a wealthy man, a capitalist' < H *pūṁjī* 'funds, capital, assets, money' (McGregor 640).

By means of Hindi suffix *-ī*, feminine abstract nouns (often pleonastic in character) are formed from the nouns with *-dār*, e.g.: *nātedārī* 'relationship' < H *nātedār* '*adj.* & *m.* related; a relative' < H *nātā* 'relationship; connection, alliance' (McGregor 552). The whole block *-dārī* , similarly to *-bandī*, can be also attached directly to basic nouns; in such cases a form with *-dār* does not exist, e.g.: *āpasdārī* 'kinship, relationship' < *āpas* 'kindred, brotherhood, intimate group' (McGregor 88).

---

[16] Cf. Beskrovnyj V. M., *op. cit.*, p. 140.

5. -faroś.

In Persian *faroš*, *firoš* is a present stem of the verb *faroxtan*, *firūxtan* 'to sell', functioning as a noun meaning 'selling; a seller' (Steingass 924) and – as such – can become a member of compounds. In Hindi it acts as a second member of determinative compound (cf. *faroś* 'a seller' (e.g.: *kitābfaroś*, '*m.* bookseller') – McGregor 678), but for the sake of the fact that it has lost in Hindi its independence and does not occur solely, it should be considered as a suffix forming masculine names of persons selling various things, e.g.: *thokfaroś* 'a wholesale dealer' < H *thok* 'mass, quantity, total amount; wholesale goods, or trade' (McGregor 471); *bātfaroś* 'seller of tales, romancer' < H *bāt* 'sthg. said, a word…' (McGregor 722).

6. -girī, -gīrī (Barxudarov 115; Dymšic II 98; Guru II 262).

In Persian *-gīrī* (-گیری) 'a taking, a handling' < P *giriftan* 'to take, seize, catch', occurs as a last member of compounds (Steingass 1109).

In Hindi this suffix has two forms: *-gīrī* and *-girī*. It joins substantives and forms feminine abstract nouns – mainly nouns of action, names of professions, occupations, and often has a shade of condemnation or scorn, e.g.: *dāīgirī* 'midwifery, a nurse's duties' < H *dāī* 'a wet-nurse, nurse; a midwife; a woman servant' (McGregor 488); *dhobīgirī* 'the washerman's trade' < H *dhobī* 'a washerman' (McGregor 534); *uṭhāīgīrī* 'theft, dirty trick' < H *uṭhāī* 'lifting, picking up' < H *uṭhānā* 'to lift, to pick up, to cause to disappear' (McGregor 117); *netāgīrī* '*pej.* leadership, leader's position or status' < H *netā* 'a leader' (McGregor 580).

7. -gīr(ā) (Barxudarov 66; Guru II 262).

In Persian *-gīr*, that is a present stem of the verb *giriftan*, functions as a member of compounds and means 'seizing, taking, keeping, holding; a captor, taker, seizer' (Steingass 1108). In Hindi, as a suffix, *-gīr* forms agent nouns and names of items having a quality described by the basic word, e.g.: *gacgīr* 'a plasterer' < H *gac* 'mortar, cement, plaster' (McGregor 250); *āṛgīr* 'partition, bulkhead; balk, boundary strip' < H *āṛ* 'covering, screen, shelter, protection, refuge' (McGregor 82). Words created by *-gīr* can become a subject to morphologisation, attaching a masculine ending *-ā*, e.g.: *uṭhāīgīrā* 'a pilferer, petty thief, a rascal' (McGregor) < H *uṭhāī* 'lifting, picking up' < H *uṭhānā* 'to lift, to pick up, to cause to disappear' (McGregor 117).

8. -kaś(ī) (Beskrovnyj 146).

In Persian *-kaš* (contemporary form *-keš*) is a present stem of the verb *kašīdan* (cont. *kešīdan*), used as the last member of compounds, meaning 'drawing, pulling, carrying, bearing, who draws, a drawer, drawer' (Steingass 1030; Pejsikov 100). In Hindi it acts as a suffix of masculine nouns of agency, names of instruments, e.g.: *kandlākaś* 'a master preparing gold or silver wire' < *kandlā* 'an ingot of gold or silver; gold or silver wire' (McGregor 154); *dhuāṁkaś* 'flue, chimney, funnel, smoke-stuck' < *dhuāṁ* 'smoke; vapour; gas' (McGregor 530). The suffix *-kaś* can attach a feminine suffix of abstract nouns *-ī*, e.g.: *phāṁkākaśī* 'hunger, starvation' < *phaṁkā* 'a mouthful; the act of tossing sthg. into the mouth' (McGregor 680).

9. -k͟hānā (Barxudarov 117; Dymšic II 95; Guru II 263).

In Persian the noun *xāna* means 'house, dwelling, habitation, etc.' (Steingass 444) and often occurs as a second component of compound names of places.

In Hindi it does not occur as an independent part of a sentence, having preserved its substantival value only in compound words (*tatpuruṣa*), where it usually stands as the first, determining member (e.g.: a Persian loan-word *k͟hānā-k͟harabī* 'ruin of the family' and a hybrid compound *k͟hānāpurī* 'filling in sections (of a form)', etc. (McGregor 235)).

However, when it joins substantives, it functions as a suffix, forming mostly masculine names of places, e.g.: *pothīk͟hānā* 'a library, book-depository' < H *pothī* 'a book, volume' (McGregor 648); *būcaṛk͟hānā* 'a slaughter-house' < E *butcher*. The increasing suffixalisation of *-k̲h̲ānā* in Hindi, however, can be proved by a noun *chāpāk̲h̲ānā*, *chāpek̲h̲ānā* 'a printing firm, printing works' < H *chāpā* 'a stamp, imprint, copy; a wooden stamp' (McGregor 342) and a word *cauk̲h̲ānā*, *cārk̲h̲ānā* '*adj.* chequered, checked; consisting of lines intersecting at right angles (a design); *m.* chequered cloth, checked muslin, cloth ornamented with squares' < H *cau-*, *cār-* 'four' (McGregor 311, 331). In these words *-k̲h̲ānā* does not mean a building anymore, but has a much more abstract sense. There are a few more nouns, which do not indicate a building, but a place in general, e.g.: *kūṛāk̲h̲ānā* 'public rubbish-dump' < H *kūṛā* 'rubbish, sweepings, dirt' (McGregor 211); *katvārk̲h̲ānā* 'scrap-heap; a rubbish-dump' < H *katvār* 'public rubbish-dump'.

10. -k̲h̲or(ī), -k̲h̲or(ā) (Barxudarov 113; Dymšic II 92; Guru II 262).

In Persian compounds *x^{w}ur-*, a present stem of the verb *x^{w}urdan* 'to eat', means 'eating, devouring, consuming' (Steingass 482).

In Hindi it plays the role of the suffix forming masculine nouns of agency and – rarely – adjectives, e.g.: *ghūsk̲h̲or* '*m.* one who takes bribes' < H *ghūs* 'a bribe, a gift, consideration' (McGregor 291); *ghamk̲h̲or* '*adj.* greenhouse (plant)' < H *ghamānā* 'to warm (in the sun)' (McGregor 285).

Sometimes the words with *-k̲h̲or* take Hindi masculine inflexion *-ā*, e.g.: *akal-k̲h̲urā* '*adj.* proud, haughty, egoist' < *akal-* 'alone' (McGregor 9), or feminine suffix of abstract nouns *-ī*, e.g.: *ghūsk̲h̲orī* 'bribery, bribe-taking' < H *ghūsk̲h̲or* (see above).

11. -navīs(ī) (Guru II 262).

A Persian word *navīs* 'writing, describing; a write' < *nivištan* 'to write' (Steingass 1436) occurs in Hindi in a few hybrid words denoting persons connected somehow with writing, e.g.: *ciṭnavīs* '*m. hist.* writer' < H *ciṭ* 'a piece of paper, *esp.* one written on' (McGregor 315); *kāpīnavīs* 'a copyist' < E *copy*. With attached *-ī* it can form feminine abstract nouns, e.g.: *ṭille-*

navīsī '*pej.* frivolous or degrading activity' < H *ṭillā* 'a shock, blow, thrust' (McGregor 404).

12. -nigār

This present stem of the Persian verb *nigāštan* 'to paint, embroider, draw' occurs in Persian compounds and means 'painting, painted; a picture' (Steingass 1423). In Hindi it appears in a hybrid word *kārṭūnnigār* '*m.* cartoonist' < E *cartoon.*

13. -niśīn, -naśīn (Guru II 262).

This present stem of the Persian verb *nišastan* 'to sit down, recline' in Persian compounds has a meaning 'sitting, sitting down or along with; an associate; a successor' (Steingass 1405).

In Hindi, similarly to other 'half-suffixes' of this type, it functions as a suffix, forming names of persons or adjectives, e.g.: *godnaśīn* '*m.* adopted child' < H *god* 'lap; bosom, embrace; *fig.* adoption' (McGregor 277); *gaddīniśīn* 'adj. the incumbent of a seat of office; a regent, vice-regent' < H *gaddī* 'a throne, royal seat' (McGregor 254). The suffix can attach *-ī* and then it forms feminine abstract nouns, e.g.: *gaddīniśīnī* 'accession to office'; *godnaśīnī* 'adoption' (cf. above).

14. -numā (Beskrovnyj 147; Guru II 262).

In Persian *-numā* / *-namā* is a present stem of the verb *numūdan* / *namūdan* 'to show, demonstrate' and occurs in compounds in the meaning of 'showing, pointing out; an index' (Steingass 1425).

In Hindi the suffix *-numā* appears very rarely, creating adjectives describing the quality shown by the basic word, e.g.: *guṭhlīnumā* 'baggy' < H *guṭhlī* 'stone (of a fruit)'; *gemdnumā* 'spherical' < H *gemd* 'a ball' (McGregor 275).

15. -parast(ī) (Barxudarov 113; Beskrovnyj 146; Dymšic II 92, 107).

The Persian word *parast* 'a worshipper, one who persists in his opinion' < P *parastīdan* 'to worship, adore, pray to, to serve' (Steingass 242), functions in Hindi as a suffix forming substantival adjectives with negative overtones, e.g.: *phūṭparast* 'schismatic, dissenting; *m. hist.* schismatic, dissenter' < H *phūṭ* 'bursting open, split, break; dissension, schism' (McGregor 686); *faiśanparast* '*adj.* fashionable; *m.* dandy, coxcomb' < E *fashion*.

The suffix *-parast* can attach the feminine suffix of abstract nouns *-ī*, e.g.: *phūṭparastī* 'splitting tactics' < H *phūṭparast* (see above).

16. -poś (Beskrovnyj 147; Guru II 263).

In Persian compounds, *-poš*, which is a present stem of the verb *pošīdan* (in contemporary Persian *pušidan*) 'to cover, conceal, clothe; to dress' has a meaning 'clothing, dressing, covering' (Steingass 260). In Hindi *-poś* is a suffix of similar meaning, forming masculine names of objects, e.g.: *palaṅgpoś* 'coverlet' < H *palaṅg* 'a bed' (McGregor 611) or pleonastic adjectives, e.g.: *khapṛailpoś* 'tiled (roof)' < H *khapṛail* 'a tiled roof' (McGregor 228).

17. -rasān (Beskrovnyj 147)

The Persian word *-rasān*, occurring in compounds and meaning 'bringing, producing' is a present stem of the causative verb *rasāndan* 'to follow up one thing by another; to bring or produce in succession' < *rasīdan* 'to arrive' (Steingass 575).

In Hindi it acts as a suffix of similar meaning, forming nouns of agency, e.g.: *ciṭṭhīrasān* 'deliverer of a letter, postman' < H *ciṭṭhī* 'a letter, a note' (McGregor 315)

18. -sāz(ī) (Barxudarov 117; Beskrovnyj 145; Dymšic II 92; Guru II 263; Stasik 153).

This present stem of the Persian verb *sāxtan* 'to make, form, fashion, prepare, etc.', occurs in Persian as a member of compounds, meaning 'preparing, making, effecting' (Steingass 640).

In Hindi it plays the role of quite a productive suffix, joining nouns and forming masculine nouns of agency, mainly names of occupation or profession, e.g.: *ghaṛīsāz* 'a watchmaker' < H *ghaṛī* 'an instrument to measure time, a watch, a clock' (McGregor

284); *dāṁtsāz* 'dental technician, dentist' < H *daṁt* 'tooth' (McGregor 487)[17]. The suffix *-sāz* can attach a suffix of feminine abstract nouns, e.g.: *ghaṛīsāzī* 'a watchmaker's trade or craft'.

19. -śāh(ī) (Barxudarov 114; Beskrovnyj 148; Dymšic II 92).

The Persian noun *šāh* 'a king, sovereign, emperor, monarch, prince' (Steingass 726) functions in Hindi as a borrowed noun 'king; (in chess, cards) the king' (McGregor 949) and as such becomes also a member of compounds, meaning 'royal, excellent, best or largest (of its kind)' (McGregor 949). But in Hindi it has also partly lost its substantival role and has begun acting as a 'half-suffix', joining nouns and forming masculine neologisms, with some negative shade of meaning, e.g.: *thailīśāh* 'a rich, wealthy man' < H *thailī* 'a bag, a sack; a purse' (McGregor 471); *baiṅkśāh* 'finansier' < E *bank*. Even more often a combined suffix *-śāhī* (*-śāh* + *-ī*), forming feminine abstract nouns, can be found, e.g.: *netāśāhī* 'supreme position , or status as leader' < H *netā* 'a leader' (McGregor 580); *abhijātśāhī* 'nobles' oligarchy; government of aristocracy' < H *abhijāt* 'well-born, of high rank; noble, aristocratic' (McGregor 47).

---

[17] This word looks like a linguistic calque of Persian *dandānsāz* 'a dentist' (Steingass 538); it could have also been formed from another Persian word denoting a tooth – *dand* (cf. Steingass 537), although Persian sources do not confirm such a form. However, it is highly possible that *dāṁtsāz* is an Indo-Persian hybrid word since *dāṁt* is the Hindi *tadbhava* word < S *danta* 'tooth, fang, task' (Kočergina V. A., *Sanskritsko-russkij slovaŕ*, Moskva 1978, p. 259).

Conclusion

Statistical analysis.

The group of 929 morphological hybrid words which has become the main material for this book, is presented in Appendix I, divided according to the alphabetical order of affixes. Its quantitative analysis looks as follows:

	Hybrids with Hindi formatives	Hybrids with Perso-Arabic formatives
Prefixes	9	91
Suffixes	223	64
'Half-suffixes'	26	516
TOTAL	**258**	**671**

Hybrid words created by means of native, Hindi affixes make up only 28% of the whole amount, and adequately, a group of hybrids formed by Perso-Arabic formatives comprises 72% of it. This significant disproportion is quite a surprise, and shows that processes of morphological Perso-Arabic hybridisation in Hindi are much deeper than it has usually been supposed. The most numerous group of affixes creating hybrid words consists of Persian 'half-suffixes'. This feature seems to be quite understandable, since these units, which have later changed into formatives, appeared in Hindi first as nominal parts of speech and common members of Perso-Arabic compounds and as such they were accepted by Hindi more easily than proper suffixes.

The productivity of individual affixes is depicted by the breakdown given below.

HINDI FORMATIVES		PERSO-ARABIC FORMATIVES	
1. -nā	43	1. -dār(ī)	188
2. -iyā	26	2. -bāz(ī)	122
3. -ā	25	3. be-	73
4. -ī	25	4. -band(ī)	55
5. -vālā, -vālī	22	5. -dān(ī)	31
6. -pan	18	6. -k͟hānā	29
7. -īlā	14	7. -śāh(ī)	20
8. -in	14	8. -girī, -gīrī	17
9. -vād(ī)	11	9. -k͟hor(-ā, -ī)	15
10. -ānī	8	10. -bardār(ī)	13
11. -āī	6	11. gair-	11
12. -nī	6	12. -kaś(ī)	10
13. -mār	6	13. -parast	10
14. -kaṭ(-ā, -ī)	5	14. -sāz(ī)	9
15. -(ī)karaṇ	5	15. -cī	8
16. ku-	4	16. -gīr(-ā)	8
17. -ṛā, -ṛī, -rī	4	17. -vān(ī)	7
18. prati-	3	18. -vār	6
19. ni-	2	19. -naśīn, -niśīn	6
20. -ail	2	20. -gar	5
21. -ū	2	21. bad-	4
22. -kṛt	2	22. -gār	3
23. -autā	1	23. -faroś	3
24. -tī	1	24. -navīs(ī)	3
25. -(ā)vaṭ	1	25. -numā	3
26. -dhārī	1	26. -poś	3
27. -pūrṇ	1	27. nā-	2
		28. -(i)cā, -(i)cī	2
		29. -(i)yat	2
		30. lā-	1
		31. -nigār	1
		32. -rasān	1

When analysing the above presented table, one can again observe, that the most productive affixes which form hybrid words are Persian 'half-suffixes' – *-dār(ī)* and *-bāz(ī)*. The highly surprising fact, that the remarkably common Hindi suffix *-vālā*, *-vālī* (corresponding in its function to Persian *-dār*) forms merely 22 hybrid words (that is less than 2,5%) can be explained only by the previously mentioned observation that it is so commonly used, that not all the words formed by attaching this suffix can be found in dictionaries.

Since there is a linguistic evidence of over 670 hybrid words, we can finally state, that 32 affixes of Perso-Arabic origin came into the word-formatting system of Hindi, becoming its rightful, productive components and in some cases even the most productive ones.

Brief semantic characteristics.

Similarly to Perso-Arabic loan-words, also hybrid words in Hindi, when classifying, should be divided into two fundamental groups: oral and literary. The first, caused by the necessity of communication in quotidian occasions, have originated in close mutual relations between local people and the invaders with a different language. They include such words, as names of new items brought to India by the newcomers, names of professions and occupations (often also new for the Indians), terms connected with crafts of different type, with trade, and with the army. Borrowings and hybrids of this kind were the first linguistic effect of the inter-language and inter-cultural clash of the Muslim and Indian societies and they began to appear in Hindi probably as early as the 11th-12th century.

The loan-words of the second kind appeared somewhat later and were connected with the Mughal period, when Dakhini and Urdu were becoming the languages of literature in the Courts of Muslim rulers (i.e. 14th-18th centuries). Among literary type of borrowings and hybrids we find a large number of words originating in Arabic, chiefly terms referring to different fields of science, literature, philosophy and religion, terms concerning administration and law, words referring to the ruler and his Court. Their penetration of Hindi was particularly frequent during the full bloom of Urdu poetry in Delhi and Lakhnau in the 18th century. Words belonging to this group are now used mainly in Urdu, forming the greater part of its lexical basis, but they can also be found in literary and vernacular Hindi. In our times, the Indian linguists who are in favour of Urdu in the dispute over a nation-wide language use this group of words for creating neologisms (which often are hybrid words) and enriching in this way the Urdu lexis[1].

As it was stated before, the appearance of hybrid words becomes possible when enough loan-words are already common in a borrowing language. Then these simple loans became a subject for hybridisation by means of native word-formatting elements as well as vehicles for alien formatives, which slowly become productive in the borrowing language. This is the main reason, why the hybrid words are rarely simple names of objects. Usually they are more complex derivatives – often adjectives or abstract words. Below are enumerated the main semantic groups of Perso-Arabic hybrids in Hindi.

a) hybrid names of items, e.g.: *bistarā* ‘*m.* bed, bedding’; *pyālī* ‘*f.* a small cup’; *taṅgiyā* ‘*f.* ribbon, belt’; *sandūḵrī* ‘*f.* a small box, casket’; *cūhādān, cūhedān* ‘*m.* a mouse-trap’; *rākh-dānī* ‘*f.* ashtray’;

b) hybrid names of profession/occupation, e.g.: *cakrānī, cākrānī* ‘*f.* a woman servant’; *bāvarcin* ‘*f.* a cook (female)’; *tabliyā* ‘*m.* drummer’; *asbābvālā* ‘*m.* loader, porter’; *kāṁsāgar* ‘*m.*

---

[1] This classification is partly based on the semantic typology of Perso-Arabic loan-words presented in Barannikovs’ study (cf. Barannikov A. P., Barannikov P. A., *Xindustani (xindi i urdu). Grammatičeskij očerk*, Moskva 1956, p. 59-65).

a copper-smith'; *bahlvān* '*m.* a driver of an ox-cart'; *jhāṛūbardār* '*m.* a sweeper'; *mukkebāzī f.* boxing'; *caukīdār* '*m.* watchman, guard'; *rājgīr* '*m.* a mason, builder'; *bijlīsāz* '*m.* electrician'

c) hybrid words connected with crafts, e.g.: *peśevālā* '*m.* a professional person, craftsman'; *īṁṭabandī* '*f.* 'brickwork; building in brick'; *khurbandī* '*f.* shoeing (a horse)'; *baṛhaīgirī* '*f.* carpenter's work'; *gacgīrī* '*f.* plastering; brick-laying'; *kandlākaśī* '*f.* producing a gold or silver wire'; *chāpākhānā* '*m.* a printing firm, printing works'; *dhobīkhānā* '*m.* a laundry'; *mistrīkhānā* '*m.* a workshop'; *pannīsāzī* '*f.* production of tinsel, tinfoil'

d) hybrid words connected with trade, e.g.: *badlāī* '*f.* exchange, barter'; *kharcvālā* '*m.* creditor'; *bedām* '*adj.* free of charge'; *thokband* '*m.* a wholesale dealer'; *borābandī* '*f.* a wholesale of cereal'

e) hybrid words connected with nature, e.g.: *garmāī* '*f.* heat'; *barfānī* '*adj.* icy; snowy'; *śernī* '*f.* a tigress, a lioness'; *sevārdār* '*adj.* covered with water-plants'; *royendār* '*adj.* hairy, woolly'; *ghamkhor* '*adj.* greenhouse (a plant)';

f) hybrid words referring to the army, e.g.: *bandūkdhārī* '*adj.* armed, carrying weapon'; *faujīkaraṇ* '*m.* militarisation'; *lāmbandī* '*f.* mobilisation'; *talvārbāz* '*m.* a sword-fighter';

g) hybrid words concerning politics, administration and law, e.g.: *pratisarkar* '*f.* a parallel government'; *naukarśāhīkaraṇ* '*m.* bureaucratisation'; *bīmākṛt* '*adj.* insured'; *gairmarksvādī* '*adj.* anti-Marxist'; *śantiparast* '*m.* pacifist'; *baniyāśahī* '*f.* plutocracy'; *pūṁjīśāhī* '*adj. & f.* capitalist; capitalism'; *tānāśāh* '*m.* despot, dictator'

h) abstract hybrid words and adjectives, eg.: *tarbuziyā* '*adj.* dark-green; *m.* dark-green colour'; *āvārāpan* '*m.* homelessness'; *beḍhaṅgī* '*f.* rudeness'; *cālbāzī* '*f.* deceit, fraud; intrigue'; *āpas-*

dārī '*f.* kinship, relationship'; *ghāskhorī* '*f.* a bribery-taking'; *nakhrīlā* '*adj.* coquettish, flirtatious'; *bepāp* '*adj.* sinless'; *viṣayvār* '*adj.* thematic'.

Even the first glance at this typology allows us to state, that the most numerous are hybrid words connected with various fields of everyday life and with the commonest activities of the people. In that case, referring to Barxudarovs' division, a hypothesis could be put forward, supposing that the prevailing number of Perso-Arabic hybrids in Hindi were oral in nature, i.e. created at the very first level of inter-language contact between Indians and Muslims. This statement, in turn, would prove the assumption of the early chronology of hybrid words (before 15th century), confirmed on the other hand by their vowel system. Unfortunately, the full confirmation of this hypothesis could be obtained only after detailed study of texts, which – because of the lack of such written evidence – remains practically impossible.

BIBLIOGRAPHY

Amman G., *Urdū aur uskā sāhitya* [Urdu and its liteature], Dillī 1950.

Asher R. E. (ed.), *The Encyclopedia of Language & Linguistics*, vol. I-X, Oxford 1994.

Axmanova O. S., *Slovaŕ lingvističeskix terminov*, Moskva 1966.

Bahri H., *Persian Influence on Hindi*, Allahabad 1960.

Bailey H. W., *Irano-Indica*, vol. 3, London 1948-50.

Barannikov A. P., *Xindustani (xindi i urdu)*, Moskva 1934.

Barannikov P. A., *Jazykovaja situacija v areale jazyka xindi*, Leningrad 1984.

Barxudarov A. S., *Slovoobrazovanie v xindi*, Moskva 1963.

Basham A. L. (ed.), *A Cultural History of India*, Delhi 1988

Beams J., *A Comparative Grammar of The Modern Aryan Languages of India*, vol. 1-3, London 1872.

Bednarczuk L. (ed), *Języki Indoeuropejskie*, vol. I, Warszawa 1986.

Beskrovnyj V. M., *Morfologičeskoe gibridnoe slovoobrazovanie v xindi*, [in:] *Xindi i urdu. Voprosy leksikologii i slovoobrazovanija*, Beskrovnyj V. M. (ed.), Moskva 1960.

Beskrovnyj V. M. (ed), *Xindi-russkij slovaŕ*, vol. I-II, Moskwa 1972.

Bhabha H., *The Location of culture*, London-New York 1994.

Bloomfield L., *Language*, Chicago 1984.

Bodmer F., Hogben L., *The Loom of Language*, London 1945.

Brass P. R., *Language, Religion and Politics in North India*, New York 1974.

Burton-Page J., *A gender of Loan Words in Hindi*, [in:] "Sir Ralph Turner Jubilee Volume", *Indian Linguistics*, vol. II, Madras 1958.

Burton-Page J., *Compound and Conjunct Verbs in Hindi*, "Bulletin of the School of Oriental (and African) Studies", vol. XIX, London.

Capell A., *Studies in socio-linguistics*, The Hague 1966.

Caudhari A., *Hindī vyākaraṇ kā itihās* [History of Hindi grammar], Patna 1972.

Chatterji K., *Origin and Development of Bengali Language*, Calcutta 1926.

Chatterji K., *Indo-Aryan and Hindi*, Calcutta 1969.

Chatterji S. K., *Iranianism*, Calcutta 1972.

Chatterji S. K. (ed.), *The cultural heritage of India*, vol. V, *Languages and literatures*, Calcutta 1978.

Chusein S. E., *Istorija literatury xindi*, Moskva 1961.

Craven R. C., *Indian art*, London 1991.

Crystal D., *An Encyclopedic Dictionary of Language & Linguistics*, Oxford 1993. (I)

Crystal D., *The Cambridge Encyclopedia of Language*, Cambridge 1988. (II)

Czekalska R., *A Turk of Hindustan*, "Folia Orientalia. Studia in honorem Stanislai Stachowski dicata", ed. Chmiel J., Śliwa J., vol. XXXVI, 2000.

Čxeidze T. D., *Imennoe slovoobrazovanie v persidskom jazyke*, Tbilisi 1969.

Davidova A. A., *Nekotorye voprosy glogolnogo slovoobrazovanija v jazyke xindustani*, [in:] "Učenye Zapiski Instituta Vostokovedenija AN SSSR", t. XIII, Moskva 1958.

Dubois J. et al., *Dictionnaire de linguistique*, Paris 1973.

Dvorjankov N. A. (ed), *Indijskaja i iranskaja filologija, voprosy dialektologii*, Moskva 1971.

Dymšic Z. M., *Grammatika jazyka xindi*, vol. I-II, Moskva 1986.

Èlovkov, D. I., *O složnyx glagolax v jazyke xindustani*, "Filologija Stron Vostoka", Leningrad 1963.

Fallon S. W., *New Hindustani-English Dictionary*, Banāras 1879.

Fergusson J., *A Dictionary of the Hindostan language*, London 1773.

Fludernik M., *Hybridity and Postcolonialism. Twentieth-Century Indian Literature*, Tübingen 1998.

Gatzlaff-Hälsig M., *Grammatischer Leitfaden des Hindi*, Leipzig 1978.

Gilchrist J., *A Grammar of the Hindoostanee Language or part 3rd of a System of Hindoostanee Philology*, Calcutta 1796.

Giles H., Saint-Jacques B. (eds.), *Language and Ethnic Relations*, Oxford 1979.

Gopal R., *Indian Muslims – a Political History*, Bombay 1964.

Gopal R., *Linguistic Affairs in India*, London 1966.

Grierson G. A. (ed), *Linguistic Survey of India*, vol. 9, Patna 1968.

Guru K., *Grammatika xindi* (transl. Barannikov P. A., Barannikov A. P.), vol. I-II, Moskva 1962.

Handa R. L., *History of Hindi Language & Literature*, Bombay 1978.

Hansen W., *Pawi Tron. Dramat Indii Wielkich Mogołów*, Warszawa 1980.

Harley A. H., *Colloquial Hindustani. With an Introduction by J. R. Firth*, London 1946.

Hartmann R. R. K, Stork F. C., *Dictionary of Language and Linguistics*, London 1972.

Hock H. H., Joseph B. D., *Language History, Language Change and Language Relationship. An Introduction to Historical and Comparative Linguistics*, Berlin-New York 1996.

Hockett Ch. F., *A course in modern linguistic*, New York 1959.

Hymes D. (ed.), *Pidginization and creolization of languages*, Cambridge-London 1971.

Jazayery M. A., Winter W. (eds.), *Languages and Cultures. Studies in Honor of Edgar C. Polomé*, Berlin-Amsterdam-New York 1988.

Katenina T. E., *Jazyk xindi*, Moskva 1960.

Kellog S. H., *A Grammar of the Hindi Language*, London 1938.

Kieniewicz J., *Historia Indii*, Wrocław 1980.

King Ch., *One language, two scripts. The Hindi Movement in Nineteenth Century North India*, Delhi-Calcutta-Madras, 1994.

Klein E., *A comprehensive etymological dictionary of the English language*, Amsterdam-London-New York 1971.

Kočergina V. A., *Sanskritsko-russkij slovać*, Moskva 1978.

Kuczkiewicz-Fraś A., *Persian elements in contemporary Hindi and their genesis*, "Zeszyty Naukowe UJ. Prace Językoznawcze" 1997, vol. 18 (MCCX).

Labov W., *Sociolingustic patterns*, Philadelphia 1972.

Lambton A. K. S., *Persian Grammar*, Cambridge 1960.

Lane Pole S., *Medieval India*, London 1926.

Lockwood W., *A Panorama of Indo-European Languages*, London 1983.

Majidi M. R., *Strukturelle Grammatik des Neupersichen (Fārsi)*, Bd. II *Morphologie*, Hamburg 1990.

Majumdar R. C. (ed), *The History and Culture of the Indian People*, vol. V and VI, Bombay 1970.

Masica C. P., *The Indo-Aryan Languages*, Cambridge 1993.

Matthews P.. H., *Oxford concise dictionary of linguistics*, Oxford 1997.

McGregor R. S., *Hindi literature from its beginning to the Nineteenth century*, Wiesbaden 1984.

McGregor R. S., *The Oxford Hindi-English Dictionary*, New Delhi 1997.

McGregor R. S., *Outline of Hindi Grammar*, Delhi 1999.

Meetham A. R., Hudson R. A., *Encyclopaedia of Linguistics, information and control*, Oxford 1969.

Meillet A., *Zarys gramatyki porównawczej języków indoeuropejskich*, Warszawa 1919.

Narula S. S., *Scientific History of Hindi Language*, New Delhi 1955.

Onions C. T. (ed.), *The Oxford dictionary of English etymology*, Oxford 1966.

Pey M. A., Gaynor F., *A Dictionary of linguistics*, New York 1954.

Pejsikov L. S., *Leksikologija sovremennogo persidskogo jazyka*, Moskva 1975.

Pejsikov L. S., *Očerki po clovoobrazovaniju persidskogo jazyka*, Moskva 1973.

Piłaszewicz S., Tulisow J. (ed), *Problemy języków Azji i Afryki*, Warszawa 1987.

Platts J. T., *Dictionary of Urdū, Classical Hindi and English*, New Delhi 1999 (1st ed. London 1884).

Platts J. T., *A Grammar of the Hindustani or Urdu Language*, London 1941.

Płusa G., *W hindi o hindi*, vol. I-III, Kraków 1986.

Pobożniak T., *Problem językowy w Indiach*, "Przegląd Orientalistyczny" 1959, vol. 2.

Rizvi S. A. A., *The wonder that was India*, vol. II, New Delhi 1995

Rubinčik Ju. A., *Persidsko-russkij slovaŕ*, vol. I-II, Moskva 1970.

Saksena B. R., *Dakhini Hindi*, Prayāg 1952.

Sapir E., *Language. An introduction to the study of speech*, New York 1921.

Sebeok Th. A., *Current Trends in Linguistics*, Hague 1969, vol. 5.

Shackle C., Snell R., *Hindi and Urdu since 1800. A common reader*, London 1990.

Shakespear J., *A Dictionary Hindūstānī and English*, London 1820.

Singer M., Cohn B.(eds.), *Structure and change in Indian society*, Chicago 1968.

Singhal D. P., *India and World Civilisation*, Part I-II, Calcutta 1993.

Sjøberg A. F., *The impact of Dravidian on Indo-Aryan: an overview*, [in:] Polomé E. C., Winter W. (eds.), *Reconstructing languages and cultures*, Berlin-New York 1992.

Small G., *A Grammar of the Urdū or Hindūstānī Language in its romanized character*, Calcutta 1895.

Stasik D., *Język hindi*, Warszawa 1998.

Steingass F., *A Comprehensive Persian-English Dicionary*, Lahore 1981.

Šamatov A. N., *Klassičeskij dakxini*, Moskva 1974.

Šamatov A. N., *Očerki istoričeskoj leksikologii xindi i urdu XV – načala XVIII vv.*, Taškent 1990.

Taylor J., *Dictionary Hindoostanee and English*, rev. by Hunter W., vol. 1-2, Calcutta 1808.

The New Encyclopaedia Britannica, vol. 6, Chicago 1990.

The Oxford English Dictionary, vol. 5, Oxford 1970.

Tivārī M., *Hindī bhāṣā par farsī aur aṅgrezī kā prabhāv* [The influence of Persian and English on the Hindi language], Varanasi 1969.

Tivārī Bh., Bālā K., *Hindī bhāṣā kī śabd-samracnā* [Word structure in Hindi], New Delhi (no date).

Trudgill P., *Dialect typology and social structure*, Trends in Linguistics, Studies & Monographs 60, New York 1992.

Turner R. L., *A Comparative Dictionary of the Indo-Aryan Languages*, London 1966.

Vajpeyi A., *Hindī par farsī kā prabhāv* [Persian Influence on Hindi], Prayāg 1958.

van Olphen H., *Religion and language varieties: the case of Hindi-Urdu*, Trends in Linguistics, Studies & Monographs 36, New York 1988.

Varmā R., *Mānak hindī koś*, vol. I-V, Prayāg 1968.

Weekes R., *Pakistan. Birth and Growth of a Muslim Nation*, Princeton 1964.

Whinnom K., *Linguistic hybridization and the 'special case' of Pidgins and Creols*, [in:] Hymes D. (ed.), *Pidginization and Creolization of Languages*, Cambridge-London 1971.

Zograf G. A., *Iranskie i arabskie èlementy v urdu*, [in:] *Xindi i urdu. Voprosy leksikologii i slovoobrazovanija*, Moskva 1960.

Zograf G. A., *Voprosy formirovania urdu*, [in:] "Učenye Zapiski Instituta Vostokovedenija AN SSSR", vol. XIII, Moskva 1958.

Zograf G. A., *Xindi, urdu i xindustani*, [in:] "Kratkie Soobščenija Instituta Vostokovedenija AN SSSR", Moskva 1956.

Zograf G. A., *Xindustani na rubeže XVIII-XIX vv*, Moskva 1961.

Appendix I

LIST OF HYBRID WORDS CREATED BY HINDI FORMATIVES

Prefixes

I. ku-

kurāh *f.* 'wrong or improper course' [Varma I 557; BXRS I 380; McGregor 207];

kurāhī *m.* 'one on a wrong course; a bad or depraved person' [Varma I 557; McGregor 207];

kurukh *adj.* 'dissatisfied, displeased' [Varma I 558; BXRS I 380; McGregor];

kusāīt *f.* 'bad or inopportune time or moment; time of trouble or distress' [Varma I 565; BXRS I 383];

II. ni-

nikhālis *adj.* 'impure, unclean' [Varma III 262; BXRS I 870];

nikharce *adv.* 'without overheads' [Varma III 262; BXRS I 870];

III. prati-

pratihazār *num.* 'per mille' [BXRS II 128];

pratisāl *adv.* 'each year, every year' [BXRS II 127];

pratisarkār *f.* 'a parallel government' [BXRS II 127];

Suffixes

I. -ā (= morphologisation of loan-words)

ablakhā *m.* 'starling' [Varma I 143; BXRS I 111];

bistarā *m.* 'bed, bedding' [BXRS II 255; McGregor 737];

caubaglā *adj.* 'four-sided, on all sides' [Varma I 290; BXRS I 555; McGregor 332];

caumahalā *adj.* 'four-storeyed' [Varma II 290; BXRS I 555; McGregor 332];

caurāhā *m.* 'a crossroads' [Varma II 292; BXRS I 556; McGregor 332];

caurāstā *m.* 'a crossroads' [Platts 447; BXRS I 556; ; McGregor 332];

cautarafā *adj.* 'four-sided' [BXRS I 554; McGregor 331];

darbā *m.* 'a fowl-house, dovecot; a hollow, or nook used for nesting'; *pej.* 'place, hole, room, cell' [Varma II 29; BXRS I 755; McGregor 480];

ekdarā *adj.* 'having a single door'; *m.* 'room, a hallway' [Varma I 397; BXRS I 284; McGregor 140];

ekmahalā *adj.* 'single-storeyed' [BXRS I 285; McGregor 140];

ekmaṃzilā *adj.* 'single-storeyed' [Varma I 398; BXRS I 285; McGregor 140];

ekrukhā *adj.* 'having a single face or side: worked or usable on one side only' [Varma I 398; BXRS I 285; McGregor 141];

ektarafā *adj.* 'one-sided; one-way (ticket); unilateral' [Varma I 396; BXRS I 284; McGregor 140];

gardanā *m.* 'the neck; a blow on the nape of the neck' [Varma II 75; BXRS I 448];

gūṁgā *adj.* *& m.* 'dumb; one who converses by signs' [Varma II 124; BXRS I 472; McGregor 273];

ikbārā *adj.* 'happening once or by chance' [Platts 1250; BXRS I 224];

jigrā *m.* 'strength, vitality, courage, pluck' [Varma II 364; BXRS I 606; McGregor 371];

kākrezā *m.* 'a piece of dark purple cloth' [Varma I 500; BXRS I 349];

marduā *m. usu. pej.* 'a man, fellow' [Varma IV 296; BXRS II 343; McGregor 794];

murgā *m.* 'a cock' [Varma IV 390; BXRS II 395; McGregor 824];

muśtabahā *adj.* 'doubtful, dubious' [Varma IV 395; BXRS II 397];

raṅg-biraṅgā *adj.* 'multicoloured, motley, diverse' [BXRS II 441; McGregor 847];

sikandrā *m.* 'semaphore' [Varma V 361; BXRS II 699];

taśtā *m.* 'a copper dish, salver' [BXRS I 701];

zambūrā *m.* 'a hornet, a large bee; a camel swivel; a kind of guitar made of two gourds' [Varma II 319; BXRS I 574];

II. -āī

badlāī *f.* 'exchange, barter; sthg. given in exchange, a replacement; price of exchange' [Platts 140; BXRS II 209; McGregor 704];

garmāī *f.* 'heat; becoming warm' [Varma II 76; McGregor 256];

muglāī *adj.* 'of Mughal style (dress, art, etc.)' [Varma IV 382; BXRS II 389 ; McGregor 820];

narmāī *f.* 'softness, pliancy; mildness, easiness (of manner), want of firmness; moderateness (of price), reduction in prices; slackness (of a trade)' [Varma III 218; BXRS I 850];

sardāī *f.* 'a cool drink' [Platts 653; BXRS II 665; McGregor 993];

turśāī *f.* 'sourness, acidity; ill-tempered' [Varma II 565; BXRS I 722; McGregor 458];

III. -ail

dagail *adj.* 'marked, spotted, stained' [Varma III 18; BXRS I 749; McGregor 475];

gusail, **gussail** *adj.* 'quick-tempered' [Varma II 123; BXRS I 471; McGregor 273];

IV. -ānī

cakrānī, **cākrānī** *f.* 'a woman servant' [Varma III 190; BXRS I 507; McGregor 296];

hinduānī *f.* 'an Indian woman' [BXRS II 809];

mehtrānī *f.* 'a sweeper's wife; a woman sweeper' [Varma IV 415; BXRS II 411; McGregor 833];

muglānī *f.* 'a woman of a Mughal class; the wife of a Mughal; female attendant (in women's apartment); sempstress' [Platts 1051; Varma IV 382; BXRS II 389; McGregor 820];

mullānī *f.* 'the wife of a *mullā*; a learned Muslim woman, schoolmistress' [BXRS II 397; McGregor 826];

naukrānī *f.* 'a woman servant' [Varma III 330; BXRS I 904; McGregor 582];

turkānī *f.* 'a Turkic or Muslim woman' [Platts 319; BXRS I 721];

ustānī *f.* 'the wife of a teacher; a woman teacher' [Varma I 385; BXRS I 276];

V. -autā

zamnautā *m.* 'a small percentage paid to one who is surety for some amount' [Varma II 333; BXRS I 585; McGregor 358];

VI. -ī

afīmī *adj.* 'having to do with opium'; *m.* 'opium-eater, opium-addict' [Varma I 142; BXRS I 111; McGregor 45];

balvāī *m.* 'rioter, rebel' [Varma IV 84; BXRS II 220; McGregor 712];

barfānī *adj.* 'icy; snowy, snow-covered' [Platts 174; BXRS II 218; McGregor 711];

bāvarcinī *f.* 'a cook (female)' [Platts 128; BXRS II 245; McGregor 728];

bidāī *f.* 'dismissal; permission to depart, taking leave; departure; gift given to one departing' [Varma IV 133; BXRS II 251; McGregor 733];

biryānī *f.* 'sthg. roasted or fried: a dish of meat and fried rice' [Platts 151; McGregor 734];

cauhaddī *f.* 'boundary, boundaries of an area' [Varma II 292; BXRS I 556; McGregor 332];

cehraī *adj.* 'flesh-coloured'; *f.* 'a flesh-coloured paint' [BXRS I 548];

dārogāī *f.* 'the office, or duties of a *dārogā* (a police inspector or superintendent)' [Varma III 53; BXRS I 771; McGregor 492];

gumānī *adj.* 'suspicious, doubting; proud' [Varma II 116; BXRS I 468; McGregor 271];

gunāhī *m.* 'a sinner'; *f.* 'sinfulness, guiltiness' [Varma II 114; BXRS I 467];

kasratī *adj.* 'taking physical or athletic exercise; developed (the body) by training or exercise; athletic, gymnastic' [Platts 833; Varma I 491; BXRS I 343; McGregor 182];

kinārī *f.* 'edging, trimming (of gold or silver)' [Varma I 529; BXRS I 367; McGregor 196];

lagamī *f.* 'a muzzle' [Varma IV 548; BXRS II 489];

madī *adj.* 'female'; *f.* 'a female' [Varma IV 337; Platts 979; BXRS II 362];

mardaī *f.* 'manliness, bravery, courage, prowess' [BXRS II 342];

matlabī *adj.* 'self-seeking, self-interested' [Varma IV 274; BXRS II 331; McGregor 786];

muṁhzorī *f.* 'hardness of mouth, headstrongness, abusiveness' [Platts 1082; Varma IV 374; BXRS II 384; McGregor 819];

murgī *f.* 'a hen, fowl' [Varma IV 390; BXRS II 396; McGregor 824];

pyālī *f.* 'a small cup or glass, a cup' [Platts 294; BXRS II 111; McGregor 651];

riyāsatī *adj.* 'pertaining to a state' [Varma IV 511; BXRS II 469; McGregor 865];

sardaī *adj.* 'greenish-yellow (as a melon called *sardā*)'; *f.* 'a greenish-yellow colour' [Platts 653; Varma V 297; BXRS II 665; McGregor 993]

śīśī *f.* 'a small glass bottle, flask' [Varma V 181; BXRS II 60-4; McGregor 552];

tandūrī *adj.* 'baked in *tandūr* (a kind of clay oven for baking bread)' [Varma II 492; BXRS I 681; McGregor 431];

vāpsī *adj.* 'return (as ticket)'; *f.* 'returning, return; giving back, refund; sending back or home; remand; a return ticket' [Varma V 35; BXRS II 536;' McGregor 914];

VII. -īlā

barfīlā *adj.* 'icy; snowy, snow-covered' [BXRS II 216; McGregor 711];

dagīlā *adj.* 'marked, spotted, stained' [BXRS I 749; McGregor 475];

dardīlā *adj.* 'painful' [Varma III 28; BXRS I 758; McGregor 482];

garmīlā *adj.* 'warm' [BXRS I 450];

jośīlā *adj.* 'passionate, ardent, zealous' [Varma II 390; BXRS I 624; McGregor 383];

kharcīlā *adj.* 'extravagant (a person), expensive (an object)' [Varma II 15; BXRS I 416; McGregor 231];

nakhrīlā *adj.* 'coquettish, flirtatious' [Varma III 203; BXRS I 843];

naśīlā *adj.* 'intoxicated; intoxicating (drink); drowsy, drooping (eyes)' [Varma III 226; BXRS I 854; McGregor 547];

pecīlā *adj.* 'twisted, coiled; involved, complicated' [Varma III 566; BXRS II 99; McGregor 643];

ragīlā *adj.* 'stringy, veiny, sinewy' [Varma IV 466; BXRS II 446];

robīlā *adj.* 'imposing, domineering' [Varma IV 532; BXRS II 483; McGregor 873];

surmīlā *adj.* 'of the colour of antimony; dark shade of grey' [BXRS II 725];

śarmīlā *adj.* 'bashful, sky; modest; ashamed' [Varma V 148; BXRS II 591; McGregor 944];

zahrīlā *adj.* 'poisonous, venomous' [Varma II 350; BXRS I 596; McGregor 365];

VIII. -in

bāvarcin *f.* 'a cook (female)' [Platts 128; BXRS II 245];

darzin *f.* 'a sempstress; a tailor's wife' [Varma III 28; BXRS I 755, 757; McGregor 482];

dehātin *f.* 'a village woman' [BXRS I 806 ; McGregor 512];

halvāin *f.* 'a wife of a sweet-maker' [Varma V 530; BXRS II 793; McGregor 1064];

k̲aidin *f.* 'a female prisoner' [BXRS I 391; McGregor 214];

k̲h̲avāsin *f.* 'a *rānī*'s lady's maid' [BXRS I 417];

mālikin *f.* 'landlady, owner' [BXRS II 370];

mazdūrin *f.* 'a woman labourer' [BXRS II 326; McGregor 783];

mehmānin *f.* 'a female guest' [Varma IV 416; BXRS II 411];

pañjābin *f.* 'a Panjabi woman' [BXRS II 12; McGregor 587];

sardārin *f.* 'leader's wife; wife of a Sikh (term of address or reference); a Sikh woman' [Platts 653; BXRS II 665; Mc-Gregor 990];

turkin *f.* 'a Turkic woman, a woman from Turkestan; a Muslim woman' [Varma II 563; BXRS I 722; McGregor 458];

yahūdin *f.* 'a Jewess' [BXRS II 429; McGregor 842];

zamīndārin *f.* 'a wife of *zamīndār*' [Platts 617]

IX. -iyā

bagiyā *f.* 'a small garden' [Platts 162; Varma IV 48; BXRS II 199; McGregor 697];

balaiyā *f.* 'misfortune, calamity, affliction' [Varma IV 86; BXRS II 221; McGregor 713];

bāliśtiyā *m.* 'a tiny dwarf' [Platts 125; BXRS II 245; McGre-gor 727];

cak̲h̲iyā *adj.* 'quarrelsome, ridiculous' [Varma II 195; BXRS I 510];

capaṛ-k̲anātiyā *m.* 'a flatterer'; *adj.* 'sordid' [Platts 422];

caugośiyā *adj.* 'four-cornered, square'; *m.* 'a square' [Varma II 287; BXRS I 553];

futūriyā, fatūriyā *adj. & m.* 'dispersed, ruined, undone; exciting quarrels, contentious, litigious; a contentious or litigious person' [Platts 776; Varma IV 25; BXRS II 164];

gardaniyāṁ *f. pl.* 'throwing sb. out by the scruff of his neck, ejection' [Varma II 75; BXRS I 448];

hisābiyā *adj.* 'calculating (a person); *m.* one who works with accounts or figures: accontant; mathematician' [Varma V 555; BXRS II 814; McGregor 1075];

jāliyā *m.* 'a forger' [Varma II 363; BXRS I 605; McGregor 370];

kamāniyā *adj.* 'arched, bent, bowed; having a spring or springs (as a bed-frame, or a mattress)'; *m.* 'archer' [Varma I 458; BXRS I 323];

k̲ānūniyā *m.* 'a legalistic or litigious person' [Varma I 508; BXRS I 353; McGregor 189];

k̲h̲asiyā *m.* 'a castrated animal (*esp.* a goat)'; *adj.* 'castrated' [Varma II 22; BXRS I 418];

lifāfiyā *adj.* 'showy, ostentatious' [Varma IV 583; BXRS II 507; McGregor 896];

madiyā *adj.* 'female (bird, animal, etc.)' [Varma IV 279; BXRS II 333];

matlabiyā *adj.* 'self-seeking, self-interested' [Varma IV 274; BXRS II 331; McGregor 786];

mazāk̲iyā *adj. usu. inv.* 'humorous' [Varma IV 269; BXRS II 328; McGregor 784];

mug̲liyā *adj. inv.* 'having to do with the Mughals' [Varma IV 382; BXRS II 389; McGregor 820];

puliyā *f.* 'a small bridge; a culvert, drainage pipe' [Platts 269; BXRS II 88; McGregor 639];

rabābiyā *m.* 'a player of the *rabāb*' [Varma IV 475; BXRS II 451; McGregor 854];

savāliyā *adj.* 'questioning, interrogative' [Varma V 313; BXRS II 675; McGregor 996];

sitāriyā *m.* 'one who plays on the *sitār*' [Platts 637; Varma V 364; BXRS II 701];

tabliyā *m.* 'drummer' [Varma II 509; BXRS I 692; McGregor 438];

taṅgiyā *f.* 'ribbon, belt' [Varma II 490; BXRS I 680];

tarbūziyā *adj.* 'dark-green'; *m.* 'dark-green colour' [Varma II 515; BXRS I 695];

tibbiyā *adj.* 'medical, medicinal' [BXRS I 715];

X. -kaṭ(-ā, -ī)

dumkaṭā *adj.* 'docked, tailed' [BXRS I 790; McGregor 503];

girahkaṭ *m.* 'a cutpurse, pickpocket' [Varma II 102; BXRS I 460; McGregor 265]

girahkaṭī *f.* 'stealing (sb's pocket), theft' [BXRS I 460];

gulkaṭ *m.* 'a stamp for printing flower patterns on cloth' [Varma II 119; BXRS I 469];

jebkaṭ *m.* 'a pickpocket' [Varma II 383; BXRS I 620; McGregor 380];

XI. -nā

āzmānā *v.t.* 'to test, to try, to examine; to try conclusions with (a person)' [Varma I 254; BXRS I 180; McGregor 82];

bagliyānā *v.t. colloq.* 'to shift (sthg.) out of the way' [Varma IV 48; BXRS II 199; McGregor 697];

bajānā *v.t.* 'to perform, to carry out in full (an order etc.)' [Platts 134; Varma IV 52; BXRS II 202; McGregor 698];

bakhiyānā *v.t.* 'to stitch' [Platts 138; Varma IV 46; BXRS II 198; McGregor 696];

bakhśānā (I caus.) *v.t.* 'to cause to give' [Platts 137; Varma IV 47; BXRS II 198; McGregor 696];

bakhśnā *v.t.* 'to bestow; to forgive' [Platts 137; Varma IV 47; BXRS II 198; McGregor 696];

bakhśvānā (II caus.) *v.t.* 'to cause to be forgiven, to obtain forgiveness (for oneself)' [Platts 137; Varma IV 47; BXRS II 198; McGregor 696];

bistarnā *v.t.* 'to spread, to extend' [Varma IV 142; BXRS II 255];

dafnānā *v.t.* 'to bury' [Varma III 21; BXRS I 750; McGregor 476];

dagnā *v.i.* 'to be branded (with an iron), to be marked (as with smallpox); to be fired (a firearm)' [Varma III 18; BXRS I 748; McGregor 474];

dāgnā (I caus.) *v.t.* 'to burn, *esp.* with an iron, to brand, to cauterise; to mark; to fire (a firearm), to shoot (a goal); to detonate; to start (a combustion engine)' [Varma III 46; BXRS I 767; McGregor 475];

farmānā *v.t.* 'to order to command'; *hon.* 'to be pleased to say (in reference to another's remarks or requests)' [Platts 779; Varma IV 9; BXRS II 166; McGregor 677];

farknā *v.t.* 'to become detached, to come apart, to separate, to loose touch' [Varma IV 8; BXRS II 165];

garknā *v.i.* 'to sink; to disappear, to be lost' [Varma II 63];

gandolnā *v.t.* 'to make foul, to pollute, to disgrace' [Varma II 54; BXRS I 438];

gardānnā *v.t.* 'to go through or over, to repeat (as a lesson)' [Varma II 75; BXRS I 448; McGregor 256];

garmānā *v.i.* 'to become warm or heated or hot; to be or become angry' [Varma II 76; BXRS I 448; McGregor 256];

gumnā *v.i.* 'to lose, to hide' [Varma II 116; BXRS I 467];

guzarnā *v.i.* 'to pass, to make one's way (past); to elapse (time), to befall' [Varma II 108; BXRS I 463; McGregor 267];

k̲abūlnā *v.i.* 'to accept, to agree' [Varma I 454; BXRS I 319; McGregor 167];

kamānā *v.t.* 'to diminish, to lessen, to abate' [Varma I 457; BXRS I 323];

kamnā *v.i.* 'to reduce, to decrease, to moderate, to relax, to deduct' [Varma I 455; BXRS I 321];

k̲h̲arādnā *v.t.* 'to turn (on a lathe); to trim' [Varma II 17; BXRS I 415; McGregor 230];

k̲h̲arcnā *v.t.* 'to spend; to use, to bring into use' [BXRS I 415; Varma II 15; McGregor 231];

k̲h̲arīdnā *v.t.* 'to buy; to bring upon oneself' [Varma II 18; BXRS I 416; McGregor 231];

laraẓnā *v.i.* 'to shake, quiver, tremble quake, totter' [Platts 955; Varma IV 563; BXRS II 496];

larzānā (I caus.) *v.t.* *reg.* 'to cause to shake, or to tremble' [McGregor 887];

mastānā *v.i.* 'to become drunk; to grow passionate or lustful; to grow vigorous or hearty; to become puffed up with pride, conceit' [Varma IV 312; BXRS II 349; McGregor 797];

nak̲āśnā, nak̲k̲āśnā *v.i.* 'to carve (in stone, wood or metal)' [Varma III 199; BXRS I 842];

narmānā *v.t.* 'to soften; to soothe, to pacify, to assuage; to reduce (as a price)'; *v.i.* 'to become soft; to grow gentle or mild; to grow less' [Varma III 218; BXRS I 850; McGregor 545];

parkārnā *v.t.* 'to draw a circle (as with compass)' [Varma III 397; BXRS II 31];

sahamnā *v.i.* 'to feel fear' [Varma V 318; BXRS II 678; McGregor 997];

sahmānā *v.t.* 'to frighten, to terrify' [Varma V 318; BXRS II 678; McGregor 997];

sardānā *v.i.* 'to become cold, to freeze' [Platts 653; Varma V 297; BXRS II 665];

sustānā *v.i.* 'to rest; to stop (work & c.), to take a rest or break' [Varma V 426; BXRS II 729; McGregor 1032];

śarmānā *v.t.* 'to make sb. ashamed'; *v.i.* 'to feel shame; to be bashful; to be embarrassed' [Varma V 148; BXRS II 590, 591; McGregor 944];

talāśnā *v.t.* 'to search, to investigate' [Varma II 522; BXRS I 700; McGregor 433];

taṁgiyānā *v.t.* 'to tighten (as the girth of horse)' [Platts 340; BXRS 680; McGregor 431];

tarāśnā *v.t.* 'to cut, to pare, to carve, to scratch out' [Varma II 517; BXRS I 696; McGregor 441];

tunaknā *v.i.* 'to flare up (in anger), to be easily irritable' [Varma II 562; BXRS I 721; McGregor 456];

turśānā *v.i.* 'to become sour, acid' [Varma II 565; BXRS I 722; McGregor 459];

vargalānā *v.t.* 'to inveigle, to entice; to incite, to provoke' [Varma V 16; BXRS II 527; McGregor 908];

zidiyānā *v.i.* 'to be persistent, to insist (on), to be or become obstinate; to be stubborn; to be refractory (a child)' [Varma II 365; BXRS I 607; McGregor 372];

XII. -nī

faḵīrnī *f.* 'a female beggar' [Platts 783; BXRS II 161; McGregor 671];

hindnī *f.* 'an Indian woman' [BXRS II 808];

sardārnī *f.* 'leader's wife; wife of a Sikh (term of address or reference); a Sikh woman' [Platts 653; BXRS II 665; McGregor 990];

śernī *f.* 'a tigress, a lioness' [BXRS II 607; McGregor 955];

turknī *f.* 'a Turkic or Muslim woman [Platts 319; BXRS I 722]

yārnī *f.* 'female friend (of a girl); mistress' [BXRS II 432; McGregor 844];

XIII. -pan

ajnabīpan *m.* 'strangeness; unusual characteristics' [BXRS I 53; McGregor 17];

āvārāpan *m.* 'homelessness' [BXRS I 212];

bādīpan *m. med.* 'flatulence, tympanites, meteorism' [BXRS II 238];

dīvānāpan *m.* 'madness; frenzy, mania' [Varma III 78; BXRS I 785; McGregor 500];

fārsīpan *m.* 'Iranian elements (in Indian languages)' [BXRS II 175];

gandāpan *m.* 'dirt, pollution' [BXRS I 438];

gūṅgāpan *m.* 'dumbness' [BXRS I 472; McGregor 273];

kamīnāpan *m.* 'lowness, baseness' [Varma I 458; BXRS I 324; McGregor 170];

mālikpan *m.* 'a state of owner, ownership' [BXRS II 370; McGregor 809];

mas<u>kh</u>arāpan *m.* 'joking, jocularity; buffoonery' [Varma IV 309; BXRS II 348; McGregor 796];

nābāligpan *m.* 'minority (below the age), infancy' [BXRS I 861; McGregor 549];

pecīlāpan *m.* 'twisting, coiling; involving' [Varma III 566];

sādāpan *m.* 'simplicity' [Varma V 336; BXRS II 687; McGregor 1004];

śarābīpan *m.* 'addiction to alcohol' [BXRS II 590; McGregor 944];

śohdāpan *m.* 'villainy, depravity; hooliganism' [Varma V 196; BXRS II 610; McGregor 957];

urdūpan *m.* 'Urdu characteristics (as in Hindi usage)' [BXRS I 273; McGregor 132];

zahrīlāpan *m.* 'venomousness, vitriol' [BXRS I 596];

zanānāpan *m.* 'effeminacy' [Varma II 329; BXRS I 581; McGregor 356];

XIV. -ṛā, -ṛī, -rī

dārūṛā *m.* 'reg. wine, liquor' [Varma III 53; BXRS I 771];

sandū<u>k</u>ṛī *f.* 'a small box, casket' [Varma V 220; BXRS II 624];

taba<u>k</u>ṛī *f.* 'a small box, one of the bells or rattles that are let into the disc of a tambourine or timbrel' [Varma II 509; BXRS I 691];

taśtaṛī, taśtarī *f.* 'a small plate, saucer' [Varma II 524; BXRS I 701; McGregor 444];

XV. -tī

kamtī *f.* 'diminution; scarcity, lack'; *adj.* 'little, few' [Varma I 455; BXRS I 321; McGregor 168];

XVI. -ū

bāzārū *adj.* 'vulgar, coarse (as temperament, speech); crude (in manufacture)' [Platts 122; Varma IV 105; BXRS II 233; McGregor 721];

dīdārū *adj.* 'reg. good to look at, attractive (person)' [Varma III 72; BXRS I 783; McGregor 499];

XVII. -(ā)vaṭ

tarāvaṭ *f.* 'dampness, moisture, humidity; coolness, refreshing quality' [Varma II 517; BXRS I 696; McGregor 441];

XVIII. -vālā, -vālī

a<u>kh</u>barvālā *m.* 'a newspaper seller, editor or proprietor; a journalist, or reporter' [BXRS I 46; McGregor 12];

amānatvālā *m.* 'one who has deposited or assigned (goods, property)' [BXRS I 124; McGregor 52];

asbābvālā *m.* 'loader, porter' [BXRS I 157];

barābarvālā *adj.* & *m.* 'equal, adjacent, opposite; an equal' [Platts 143; BXRS II 217; McGregor 710];

bur<u>k</u>evālī *adj.* & *f.* 'wearing a *bur<u>k</u>ā* (a long veil reaching nearly to the feet, as worn by Muslim women)' [BXRS II 262; McGregor 742];

jahāzvālā *m.* 'a sailor, a seaman; a passenger of a ship' [BXRS I 597];

jāydādvālā *m.* 'possessor, owner, holder' [BXRS I 604];

jildvālā *m.* 'one who binds books' [BXRS I 609];

kamīvālā *m.* 'suffering for deficiency; poor' [BXRS I 324];

kār<u>kh</u>ānevālā *m.* 'factory-owner, industrialist' [BXRS I 357];

muhr(a)vālā *adj.* 'glazed or smoothed (paper)' [BXRS II 399];

murgīvālā *m.* 'a poultry-farmer' [McGregor 824];

nakhāsvālī *f.* 'a prostitute' [BXRS I 844];

nakāśīvālā *adj.* 'decorated with carving, sculpture etc.' [BXRS I 842];

naukrīvālā *m.* 'a servant, attendant, retainer' [BXRS I 904];

peśevālā *m. & adj.* 'a professional person, craftsman, tradesman; professional' [BXRS II 102];

raddīvālā *m.* 'one who collects and sells spoilage' [BXRS II 450];

śahrvālā *m.* 'a townsman, resident of a particular city or town' [BXRS II 593; McGregor 946];

śarmvālā *adj. & m.* 'shame-faced; bashful, shy; a shame-faced or bashful person' [Platts 725; BXRS II 591];

tandūrvālā *m.* 'a baker' [BXRS I 681];

tārvālā *adj. & m.* 'a telegraph boy, a telegraph employee; stringed (an instrument)' [BXRS I 710; McGregor 449];

umrvālā *m.* 'adult, grown up' [BXRS I 273];

Half-sufixes

I. -dharī

bandūkdhārī *adj.* 'armed, carrying weapon' [BXRS II 194];

II. -(ī)karaṇ

gairfaujīkaraṇ *m.* 'demilitarisation' [BXRS I 476];

faujīkaraṇ *m.* 'militarisation' [BXRS II 191];

mazbūtīkāraṇ *m.* 'strengthening' [BXRS II 327];

naukarśāhīkaraṇ *m.* 'bureaucratisation' [BXRS I 904; McGregor 582];

sarkārīkaraṇ *m.* 'nationalisation' [BXRS II 664];

III. -kṛt

bīmākṛt *adj.* 'insured' [BXRS II 258; McGregor 739];
gairfaujīkṛt *adj.* 'demilitarised' [BXRS I 476];

IV. -mār

dammār *m.* 'a drug-addict' [Varma III 25; BXRS I 753; McGregor 478];
jahāzmār *adj.* 'anti-aircraft' [BXRS I 597; McGregor 365];
jamāmār *m.* 'an embezzler, one who extorts money' [Varma II 334; BXRS I 586; McGregor 358];
yārmār *m.* 'one who deceives or cheats his friend or friends, a deceiver, a cheat; one who betrays his friend, a traitor' [Platts 1247; Varma IV 443; BXRS II 432];
yārmārī *f.* 'deceiving or cheating or betraying a friend' [Platts 1247; BXRS II 432];
zahrmār *adj. & m.* 'anti-toxic, antidote' [Platts 619; BXRS I 596; McGregor 365];

V. -pūrṇ

jośpūrṇ *adj.* 'passionate, ardent' [BXRS I 624; McGregor 383];

VI. -vād(ī)

carkhāvād *m.* 'one of the points of Gandhi's programme of non-cooperation' [BXRS II 517];
faujīvād *m.* 'militarism' [BXRS II 191; McGregor 690];
faujīvādī *adj. & m.* 'militarist' [BXRS II 191; McGregor 690];
gairmarksvādī *adj.* 'anti-Marxist' [BXRS I 476];

jaṅgvādī *m.* 'warmonger' [BXRS II 573];
naslvād *m.* 'racialism' [BXRS I 854; McGregor 547];
naslvādī *m.* 'racialist' [BXRS I 854; McGregor 547];
pyālāvād *m.* 'drunkenness, alcoholism' [BXRS II 110];
pyālāvādī *m.* 'drunkard, alcoholic' [BXRS II 111];
yahūdīvād *m.* 'Judaism' [BXRS II 429];
yahūdīvādī *adj.* 'Judaistic'; *m.* 'a Judaist' [BXRS II 429];

LIST OF HYBRID WORDS CREATED BY PERSO-ARABIC FORMATIVES

Prefixes

I. bad-

badcalan *adj.* 'ill-behaved, depraved, vicious' [Varma IV 61; BXRS II 207; McGregor 702];

badcalnī *f.* 'bad or wrong behaviour, depravity' [Varma IV 61; BXRS II 207; McGregor 702];

badḍaul *adj.* 'misshapen' [Platts 139; BXRS II 207; McGregor 703];

baddū *adj. & m.* 'infamous; a bad character, infamous man' [Varma IV 64; BXRS II 210];

II. be-

bearth *adj.* 'absurd, nonsensical' [Platts 201; BXRS II 265];

beās *adj.* 'depressed, despond' [BXRS II 266];

beāsar, beāsrā *adj.* 'ineffective' [BXRS II 266; McGregor 744];

bebas *adj.* 'without power or authority, helpless, weak, subject' [Varma IV 163; BXRS II 271; McGregor 745];

bebasī *f.* 'powerlessness, helplessness' [Varma IV 163; BXRS II 271; McGregor 745];

bebāt *f.* 'sthg. trivial or nonsensical (a remark, pretext)' [BXRS II 271; McGregor 745];

bebhāv *adj.* 'countless, incalculable, excessive' [Varma IV 163; BXRS II 272];

bebyāhā *adj.* 'unmarried, single' [Varma IV 163; BXRS II 272];

bebyāj *adj.* 'interest-free' [BXRS II 272];

becain *adj.* 'uneasy, restless' [Platts 202; Varma IV 159; BXRS II 268; McGregor 744];

becainī *f.* 'restlessness; alarm, alert' [Platts 202; Varma IV 159; BXRS II 268; McGregor 744];

bedāṛhī *adj.* 'beardless' [BXRS II 270; McGregor 744];

bedām *adj.* 'free of charge' [Varma IV 161; BXRS II 270; McGregor 745];

beḍaul *adj.* 'misshapen, ugly, awkward, uncouth' [Platts 203; Varma IV 160; BXRS II 269; McGregor 744];

beḍhab *adj.* 'misshapen, ugly; difficult, troublesome, reckless, uncontrollable, harsh, cruel, strange' [Platts 203; Varma IV 160; BXRS II 269; McGregor 744];

beḍhaṅg *adj.* 'uncouth' [Platts 203; Varma IV 160; BXRS II 269; McGregor 744];

beḍhaṅgā *adj.* 'disordered, chaotic, wrong-headed (approach)' [Platts 203; Varma IV 160; BXRS II 269; McGregor 744];

beḍhaṅgī *f.* 'uncouthness, rudeness' [Platts 203; McGregor 744];

bedhaṛak *adj.* 'fearless, unhesitant, confident, bold' [Platts 203; McGregor 745];

bedharm *adj.* 'unbelieving' [Varma IV 162; BXRS II 270];

bedhyānī *f.* 'upset-mindedness' [BXRS II 270];

beghar *adj.* 'homeless' [BXRS II 267; McGregor 744];

behāth *adj.* 'handless, armless, idle, helpless, beyond control' [BXRS II 275; McGregor 745];

behath(i)yār *adj.* 'unarmed' [BXRS II 275; McGregor 745];

behath(i)yārbandī *f.* 'disarmament' [BXRS II 272];

beiñjan *adj.* 'without an engine (glider)' [BXRS II 266];

bejaṛ, **bejoṛ** *adj.* 'unfounded, groundless' [Platts 202; Varma IV 159; BXRS II 268];

bejalā *adj.* 'unlit (a lamp, cigarette)' [BXRS II 268; McGregor 744];

bejhijhak *adj.* & *adv.* 'resolute, determined, daring' [BXRS II 268];

bejoṛ *adj.* 'incomparable, without joins' [Varma IV 221; BXRS II 268; McGregor 744];

bejot *adj.* & *m.* 'uncultivated (land), land left uncultivated' [Platts 202; BXRS II 268; McGregor 744];

bejūn *adj.* 'untimely' [Platts 202; BXRS II 268; McGregor 744];

bekahā *adj.* 'disobedient, naughty' [Varma IV 157; BXRS II 266];

bekām *adj.* 'useless, ineffective, worthless, without work' [Platts 203; BXRS II 266; McGregor 745];

bekāraṇ *adj.* 'causeless' [Platts 203; BXRS II 267];

bekhaṭak, bekhaṭke *adj.* & *adv.* 'free from anxiety or apprehension' [Platts 203; Varma IV 158; BXRS II 267; McGregor 744];

bekhet *adj.* 'landless (cultivator)' [BXRS II 267];

belāg, belgāv *adj.* 'unconnected, independent, inaccessible, candid, categorical (as an assurance)' [Platts 204; Varma IV 165; BXRS II 273; McGregor 745];

beman *adj.* & *m.* 'listless, apathetic; listlessness' [Varma IV 163; BXRS II 272; McGregor 745];

bemel *adj.* 'inharmonious, incompatible, incongruous' [Varma IV 163; BXRS II 272; McGregor 745];

bemilāvaṭ *adj.* 'without admixture, clean' [BXRS II 272];

benāp *adj.* 'unmeasured, unsurveyed' [Platts 204; BXRS II 271; McGregor 745];

beniyām *adj.* 'not in order, irregular, improper' [Platts 204; BXRS II 271];

bepaṛhā-likhā *adj.* 'illiterate' [BXRS II 271; McGregor 745];

bepaindī *adj.* 'without a base: wavering (in attitudes, opinions)' [BXRS II 271; McGregor 745];

bepaisā *adj.* 'penniless, without money' [BXRS II 271];

bepāp *adj.* 'sinless' [BXRS II 271];

bepatā *adj.* 'of unknown whereabouts: missing (a person), lost (a thing, undeliverable (a letter)' [BXRS II 271; McGregor 745] – cf. **lāpatā**;

1. bepīr *adj.* 'without a spiritual mentor' [Varma IV 162; BXRS II 271; McGregor 745];

2. bepīr *adj.* 'unfeeling, merciless' [Varma IV 162; BXRS II 271; McGregor 745];

beras *adj.* 'unjuicy; tasteless, dull' [Varma IV 163; BXRS II 272];

berok, **berokṭok** *adj.* 'unhindered, unrestrained'; *adj. m.* 'unemployed, unemployed person' [Platts 203; Varma IV 164; BXRS II 272; McGregor 745];

berūp *adj.* 'plain, unsightly' [Varma IV 164; BXRS II 272];

besahārā *adj.* 'helpless, powerless' [BXRS II 274];

besamajh *adj.* 'unintelligent, stupid' [Platts 203; Varma IV 167; BXRS II 274; McGregor 745];

besamajhī *f.* 'stupidity, unreason' [Varma IV 167; BXRS II 274; McGregor 745];

besamay *adj.* 'untimely' [BXRS II 274];

besaṁbhāl *adj.* 'careless, unconscious' [Varma IV 166; BXRS II 274];

besirpair *adj.* 'absurd, ridiculous' [BXRS II 275; McGregor 745];

besoce(-samjhe) *adj.* 'thoughtlessness, heedlessness' [Platts 203; BXRS II 275; McGregor 745];

besudh *adj.* 'unconscious, beside oneself (with joy or grief)' [Varma IV 167; BXRSII 275; McGregor 745];

besudhī *f.* 'unconsciousness; confusion' [Varma IV 167; BXRSII 275; McGregor 745];

besur, **besurā** *adj.* 'out of tune, discordant' [Varma IV 167; BXRS II 275; McGregor 745];

besure *adv.* 'out of tune, discordantly' [BXRS II 275];

besvād *adj.* 'insipid, tasteless, dull' [BXRS II 275];

betālā, **betāl** *adj.* 'out of time (in music), out of time, rhythm' [Platts 202; Varma IV 161; BXRS II 269; McGregor 745];

beṭhaur *adj.* 'out of place, improper' [Platts 202; BXRS II 268; McGregor 744];

beṭhīk *adj.* 'unsatisfactory, wrong' [BXRS II 268; McGregor 744];

beṭhikānā *adj.* 'having no resting-place, homeless, not to be depended on, uncertain, pointless' [Platts 202; McGregor 744];

beṭhikāne *adv.* 'unfounded, out of place' [Varma IV 160; BXRS II 268; McGregor 744];

beṭikaṭ *adj.* 'ticketless (travel)' [BXRS II 268; McGregor 744];

betukā *adj.* 'unrhyming, not assonating, without rhyme or reason, pointless, uncouth' [Varma IV 161; BXRS II 269; McGregor 744];

betukī *f.* 'a senseless remark' [BXRS II 270; McGregor 744];

III. gair-

gairfaujīkaraṇ *m.* 'demilitarisation' [BXRS I 476];

gairfaujīkṛt *adj.* 'demilitarised' [BXRS I 476];

gairhathiyārbandī *f.* 'disarmament' [BXRS I 476];

gairhindī-bhāṣī *adj.* 'not a Hindi native-speaker' [BXRS I 476];

gairjānkārī *f.* 'lack of knowledge or familiarity' [BXRS I 475; McGregor 275];

gairkhilāṛī-kaptān *m.* 'a captain of the team that does not take part in the match' [BXRS I 475];

gairlaṛākā *m.* 'civilian' [BXRS I 476];

gairlohā *m.* 'non-ferrous metal' [BXRS I 476];

gairmarksvādī *adj.* 'anti-Marxist' [BXRS I 476];

gairrājnītik *adj.* 'apolitical, politically indifferent' [BXRS I 476];

gairvargīy *adj.* 'classless' [BXRS I 476];

V. lā-

lāpatā *adj.* 'lost; wasted; without an address' [Varma IV 574; BXRS II 502] – cf. **bepatā**;

VI. nā-

nāsamajh *adj.* 'foolish, unintelligent' [Varma III 253; BXRS II 866; McGregor 549];

nāsamajhī *f.* 'foolishness, lack of intelligence, misunderstanding' [Varma III 253; BXRS II 866; McGregor 549];

Suffixes

I. -(i)cā, -(i)cī

ḍolcā, ḍolcī *m.* 'a bucket'; *f.* 'a small bucket, a small basket' [Varma II 477; BXRS I 673; McGregor 423];

sīṅkcā *m.* 'window bars' [BXRS II 711];

II. -cī

afīmcī *m.* 'opium-eater; one who takes opium for excitement as a habit' [Platts 63; Varma I 142; BXRS I 111; McGregor 45];

bigulcī *m.* 'a man playing *bigul* [E bugle]; in army' [Varma IV 128];

bhaṅgercī *m.* 'a habiyual drinker of *bhaṅg*; one who is addicted to drinking *bhaṅg*' [Platts 193];

ḍhaṇḍhorcī, ḍhiṇḍhorcī *m.* 'a public crier' [Varma II 479; BXRS I 675, 677; McGregor 425];

golcī *m.* 'a goal-keeper' [BXRS I 481; McGregor 279];

madakcī *m.* 'crazy; drug-addict; person intoxicated by alcohol, *bhaṅg*, opium, etc.' [Varma IV 277; BXRS II 332; McGregor 787];

miḍilcī *m. also pej.* 'one who has finished a middle school' [Varma IV 357; BXRS II 373];

rāyfalcī *m.* 'a rifleman' [BXRS II 464];

III. -dān(ī)

bālūdānī *f.* 'a sand-pit' [Varma IV 121; BXRS II 245];

battīdān *m.* 'candlestick, chandelier' [BXRS II 206];

cūhādān, cūhedān *m.* 'a rat-trap, mouse-trap' [Varma II 273; BXRS I 547; McGregor 328];

cūhedānī *f.* 'a rat-trap, mouse-trap' [Varma II 173; BXRS I 547];

cūnādānī, cūnedānī *f.* 'a box for holding the lime which is eaten with betel or tobacco' [Varma II 171; BXRS I 546];

dhuāṁdān *m.* 'outlet (in a roof) for smoke; chimney' [Varma III 175; BXRS I 830; McGregor 530];

dhūpdān *m.* 'a censer, container for incense' [Varma III 180; BXRS I 832; McGregor 532];

dūdhdānī *f.* 'a vessel for milk' [BXRS I 796; McGregor 507];

gilaurīdān *m.* 'a small box for holding betel' [Varma II 105; BXRS I 461];

gonddānī *f.* 'a gum- or glue-bottle' [Varma II 132; McGregor 276];

hulāsdānī *f.* 'a snuff-box' [Varma V 562; BXRS II 818; McGregor 1077];

kaṭordān *m.* 'a metal vessel with a cover' [Varma I 435; BXRS I 308; McGregor 159];

kāmdān, kāmdānī *f.* 'a type of embroidery on net or muslin (small flowers worked in gold or silver thread)' [Varma I 512; BXRS I 355; McGregor 190];

kūṛedān *m.* 'rubbish-din' [BXRSI I 385; McGregor 211];

macchardānī *f.* 'mosquito-net' [Varma IV 267; BXRS II 326; McGregor 782];

masidān *m.* 'an ink-pot' [Platts 1036; BXRS II 349];

masidānī *f.* 'an ink-pot' [Varma IV 310; BXRS II 349];

missīdān *m.* '*missī*-box [*missī* = a kind of powder used cosmetically to stain the teeth or lips black]' [BXRS II 378; McGregor 814];

missīdānī *f.* '*missī*-box' [BXRS II 378; McGregor 814];

muśdān *m.* 'mousetrap' [BXRS II 405];

musdānī, muśdānī *f.* 'mousetrap' [BXRS II 405];

nāsdān *m.* 'snuff-box' [Varma III 253; BXRS I 866; McGregor 555];

pāndān *m.* 'container for betel-leaf' [Varma III 478; BXRS II 64; McGregor 622];

pāvdān *m.* 'foot-rest, running-board, gangway' [Varma III 494; BXRS II 72; McGregor 626];

phūldān *m.* 'receptacle for flowers' [Varma IV 30; BXRS II 185; McGregor 687];

pīkdān *m.* 'spittoon' [Varma III 514; BXRS II 79; McGregor 632];

rākhdānī *f.* 'ashtray' [BXRS II 457; McGregor 859];

sindūrdānī *f.* 'vermilion-box' [BXRS II 698; McGregor 1011];

siṅgārdān *m.* 'toilet-case' [Varma V 357; BXRS II 697; McGregor 1011];

tildānī, tiledānī *f.* 'container for small objects, a sewing-bag' [Varma II 553, 554; BXRS 717; McGregor 453];

ugāldān *m.* 'spittoon' [Varma I 319; BXRS I 238; McGregor 114];

IV. -gar

gacgar *m.* 'plasterer' [Varma II 59; BXRS I 439];

kāṁsāgar *m.* 'copper-smith' [Varma I 499; BXRS 348];

kundīgar *m.* 'a fuller of cloth' [Varma I 541; BXRS I 373; McGregor 201];

phāṁsīgar *m.* 'strangler, executioner'; *hist.* 'thug' [Platts 283];

sīsāgar *m.* 'a person working in lead; boiler-smith' [BXRS II 715];

V. -gār

chāpāgār *m.* 'a cloth-printer' [BXRS I 564];

kāmgār *m. & adj.* 'a labourer, working, having work' [Varma I 512; BXRS I 355];

phāṁsīgār *m.* 'strangler, executioner'; *hist.* 'thug' [Platts 283; BXRS II 173; McGregor 680];

VI. -vān(ī)

bahlvān *m.* 'a driver of an ox-cart' [BXRS II 224; McGregor 715];

ḍyoṛhīvān *m.* 'door-keeper, porter' [Varma II 478; BXRS I 674; McGregor 424];

ekkāvān *m.* 'driver, coachman' [Varma I 401; BXRS I 287];

ekkāvānī *f.* 'carriage; transport charges' [Varma I 401; BXRS I 287];

gāṛīvān *m.* 'a carter, carman, carriage-driver, coachman' [Varma II 94; BXRS I 456; McGregor 263];

ikkevān *m.* 'a driver of *ikkā* (a one-horse vehicle)' [BXRS I 225] – cf. **ekkāvān**;

ūṁṭvān *m.* 'camel-driver' [Varma I 386; BXRS I 277; McGregor 136];

VI. -vār

bevarevār *adj.* & *adv.* 'detailed, through; minutely, in detail' [Varma IV 166; BXRS II 274];

bhāṣāvār *adj.* 'linguistic' [BXRS II 302; McGregor 766];

byorevār *adj.* 'detailed, circumstantial' [Varma IV 179; BXRS II 282; McGregor 752];

dhārāvār *adv.* 'point by point, paragraph by paragraph' [BXRS I 828];

lambarvār *adv.* 'in order, by turns' [McGregor 877];

viṣayvār *adj.* 'thematic' [BXRS II 568];

VII. -(i)yat

aṁgreziyat *f.* 'English (or western) ways; cultivation of the English language in India' [Varma I 6; BXRS I 28; McGregor 3];

gāndhīyat *f.* 'Gandhism' [BXRS I 455];

Half-suffixes

I. -band(ī)

āṛband *m.* 'the knot tying a loin-cloth; a tightly tied loin-cloth; a cloth worn by Hindus, passing round the waist and between the thighs, and fastened behind' [Varma I 256; Platts 42; McGregor 83];

borābandī *f.* 'a wholesale of cereal' [Varma IV 175; BXRS II 280];

cakbandī *f.* 'defining or marking the boundaries of a section of land; division of holdings; consolidation of holdings' [Varma II 189; BXRS I 507; McGregor 296];

caubandī *f.* 'binding, attaching at four points, shoeing (a horse); a bodice or jacket having four tie-straps' [Varma II 290; BXRS I 555; McGregor 332];

chaparband, chapparband *m.* 'a thatcher' [Varma II 299; BXRS I 260, 261];

chaparbandī, chapparbandī *f.* 'thatching, price of thatching, cultivating, with permanent residence (in a village)' [Varma II 299; BXRS I 260, 261];

1. cīrāband *f.* 'a virgin' [Varma II 259; BXRS I 539];

2. cīrāband *m.* 'one who wears the turban called *cīrā*; also one who makes such turbans' [Varma II 259; BXRS I 539];

ḍabbāband, ḍibbāband *adj.* 'preserved, caned (food)' [BXRS I 665, 670; McGregor 418];

ḍabbābandī, ḍibbābandī *f.* 'canning, preserving' [BXRS I 665, 670; McGregor 418];

dalbandī *f.* 'fractionation; division' [Varma III 34; BXRS I 760];

dhaṛābandī *f.* 'balancing, counterpoising' [Varma III 148; BXRS I 818];

dhotīband *adj.* 'wearing a *dhotī*'; *m.* 'one who wears a *dhotī*' [Platts 550; McGregor 534];

gaṛhbandī *f.* 'a fort, a stronghold castle' [BXRS I 442];

ghāṭbandī *f.* 'closure of a port; an embargo' [Varma II 166; BXRS I 495; McGregor 287];

gherābandī *f.* 'encirclement' [Varma II 177; BXRS I 501; McGregor 292];

gherbandī *f.* 'enclosed by a wall, garden' [BXRS I 501];

ghuṁghrūband *f.* 'a dancer' [Varma II 170; BXRS I 489];

guṭband, guṭṭaband *adj.* 'factional, conspiratorial' [BXRS I 464];

guṭbandī, guṭṭabandī *f.* 'a group; a faction, union' [Varma II 110; BXRS I 464];

hāthbandī *f.* 'full occupation, filling out (a period of time) with occupation' [BXRS II 804];

hathiyārband *adj.* 'armed, accoutred, equipped' [Platts 1219; BXRS II 784; McGregor 1057];

hathiyārbandī *f.* 'arming' [BXRS II 784; McGregor 1057];

īṁṭabandī *f.* 'brickwork, building in brick' [Platts 515; BXRS I 234; McGregor 109];

jakaṛband *adj.* 'tight, fast bound, well-strung' [Varma II 320; BXRS I 575];

jālband *m.* 'a carpet decorated with intertwined plants' [Varma II 362; BXRS I 605];

jattheband *adv.* 'formed into a group or band' [BXRS I 578; McGregor 354];

jatthebandī *f.* often *pej.* 'formation into a group or band' [BXRS I 578; McGregor 354];

khiṛkīband *adj.* 'rented by only one lessee' [Varma II 30; BXRS I 424];

khurbandī *f.* 'shoeing (a horse)' [Varma II 37; BXRS I 428];

laṭṭhband *adj.* 'armed with sticks or clubs' [BXRS II 492; McGregor 882];

laṛāībandī *f.* 'truce, armistice' [BXRS II 493; McGregor 833];

lāmband *adj.* 'mobilised' [BXRS II 503; McGregor 892] ;

lāmbandī *f.* 'mobilisation' [Varma IV 575; BXRS II 503; McGregor 892];

laṁgoṭband *m.* 'a strip of cloth to which the loin-cloth is fastened; one whose loin-cloth is fastened, a confirmed bachelor' [Platts 966; Varma IV 538; BXRS II 485; McGregor 876];

milbandī *f.* 'closing of a mill; lockout' [BXRS II 376];

muṁhband *adj. & m.* 'closed, corked (a bottle); a muzzle' [Varma IV 374; BXRS II 384; McGregor 818];

muniṛasāband *m. hist.* 'a servant whose duty is to tie a turban' [Varma IV 370];

nākābandī, nākebandī *f.* 'closing a road, or a frontier; collecting toil or customs blockade' [Varma III 231, 232; BXRS I 856, 857; McGregor 550];

paratbandī *f.* 'flaking, splitting into layers' [BXRS II 33; McGregor 603];

phāṭakbandī *f.* 'custody, impoundment' [Platts 282; BXRS 174; McGregor 681];

sehrābandī *f.* 'the act of garlanding a bridegroom' [Varma V 449; BXRS II 742; McGregor 1039];

sīlband *adj.* 'sealed' [BXRS 715];

sirband *m.* 'a turban' [Varma V 373; BXRS II 708];

sirbandī *f.* 'women's head-dress' [Varma V 373; BXRS II 708];

tālāband *adj.* 'locked out' [BXRS I 712; McGregor 450];

tālābandī *f.* 'lockout (of a work-force)' [Varma II 540; BXRS I 712; McGregor 450];

ṭāṅkīband *adj.* 'strengthen with metal rods' [Varma II 429; BXRS I 644];

taṛbandī *f.* 'sound of snapping or crackling' [Varma II 498; BXRS I 686];

ṭhāṭbandī, ṭhāṭarbandī, ṭhāṭhbandī *f.* 'framework (for illumination etc.)' [Platts 361; Varma II 452; BXRS I 659];

thokband *m.* 'a wholesale dealer' [BXRS I 744];

thokbandī *f.* 'a wholesale purchase' [BXRS I 744];

tukband *m.* 'a versifier' [McGregor 456];

tukbandī *f.* 'versifying' [Platts 331; Varma II 561; BXRS I 720];

vāyuband *adj.* 'hermetic, air tight' [BXRS II 537];

II. -bardār(ī)

bahaṁgībardār *m.* 'porter equipped with a *bahaṁgī* (a pole with slings at the ends for carrying loads)' [Platts 193; BXRS II 223; McGregor 714];

ballambardār *m.* 'a spearman, lancer, lance-bearer' [Varma IV 87; BXRS II 221];

barchabardār, **barchebardār** *m.* 'spearman, lancer' [Platts 146; BXRS II 215; McGregor 708];

bhālābardār *m.* 'spearman, lancer' [Varma IV 215; BXRS II 300; McGregor 765];

caranbardār *m.* 'one who carries his master's shoes, shoe-bearer' [Varma II 212; BXRS I 517];

chaṛībardār *m.* 'the marshal that walks before people of consequence with the mace or wand of office, a mace-bearer' [Varma II 216; BXRS I 559];

cilambardār *m.* 'one who prepares a *cilam* (pipe) or a *hūkka* (water-pipe)' [Varma II 255; BXRS I 537; McGregor 320];

jhaṇḍābardār *m.* 'a flag-bearer, a standard-bearer' [BXRS I 628];

jhāṛūbardār *m.* 'a sweeper' [BXRS I 634; McGregor 393];

rasoībardār *m.* 'a servant serving at the table' [Varma IV 487; BXRS II 455];

soṇṭābardār, soṇṭebardār *m.* 'a staff-bearer, macebearer, one who, in a retinue of a great personage, bears a short, curved club (generally covered with silver)' [Varma V 453; BXRS II 744];

thailībardār *m.* 'a man carrying sacks, bags from place to place' [BXRS I 744];

thailībardārī *f.* 'carrying sacks, bags; a tax for carrying bags' [Varma III 9; BXRS I 744];

III. -bāz(ī)

aiṇṭhbāz *m.* 'an ostentatious or arrogant person' [Platts 115; McGregor 144];

akaṛbāz *m.* 'an ostentatious or arrogant person' [Varma I 25; BXRS I 41; McGregor 9];

akaṛbāzī *f.* 'stiffness, hardness; crookedness; constipation; stubborness; ostentation; arrogance, conceit' [Varma I 25; BXRS I 41; McGregor 9];

akhāṛebāz *m.* 'a wrestler; an athlete'; *transf.* 'an intriguer, manoeuver' [BXRS I 46; McGregor 12];

akhāṛebāzī *f.* 'wrestling; manoeuvring' [BXRS I 46; McGregor 12];

aṇṭībāz *m.* 'a light-fingered person' [Varma I 10; BXRS I 31; McGregor 4];

aṛaṅgebāz *m.* 'an obstructive, or interfering person' [Varma I 56; BXRS I 56; McGregor 20];

aṛaṅgebāzī *f.* 'obstructiveness' [Varma I 56; BXRS I 56; McGregor 20];

aṭkalbāz *adj.* 'shrewd'; *m.* 'good guesser, appraiser' [Platts 19; BXRS I 55; McGregor 18];

aṭkalbāzī *f.* 'shrewdness; a guess, conjecture' [BXRS I 55; McGregor 18];

baiṭhakbāz *m.* 'a gossiper, intriguer' [BXRS II 277; McGregor 748];

baiṭhakbāzī *f.* 'gossiping, intriguing' [BXRS II 277; McGregor 748];

ballebāz *m.* 'batsman, batter' [BXRS II 221; McGregor 713];

ballebāzī *f.* 'batting, batsmanship' [BXRS II 221; McGregor 713];

bambāz *adj.* 'delivering bombs (as aircraft)' [Varma IV 72; BXRS II 213; McGregor 707];

bambāzī *f.* 'a bombing raid' [Varma IV 72; BXRS II 213; McGregor 707];

bāṁṛībāz *m.* 'wielder of a cudgel' [Varma IV 100; BXRS II 230; McGregor 718];

baṭerbāz *m.* 'bird-fancier, fowler' [Varma IV 54; BXRS II 203];

baṭerbāzī *f.* 'a quail-fight' [Varma IV 54; BXRS II 203];

baṭṭebāz *m.* 'juggler, trickster, humbug, cheat, swindler' [Platts 132; Varma IV 55; BXRS II 203];

baṭṭebāzī *f.* 'juggling, jugglery, sleight of hand, trickery, cheating, swindling' [Platts 132; BXRS II 203];

bevarebāzī *f.* 'deception; trick, cunning' [Varma IV 166; BXRS II 274];

byorebāz *adj.* 'shrewd, clever; cunning' [Varma IV 179; BXRS II 282; McGregor 752];

cālbāz *adj.* 'deceitful, fraudulent'; *m.* 'a deceitful person' [Varma II 235; BXRS I 528; McGregor 312];

cālbāzī *f.* 'deceit, fraud; intrigue' [Varma II 235; BXRS I 528; McGregor 312];

caṇḍūbāz *m.* 'an opium addict' [Varma II 183; BXRS I 504; McGregor 294];

chakkebāz *m.* 'a wily person' [Varma II 295; BXRS I 558; McGregor 337];

chakkebāzī *f.* 'cunning, trick' [BXRS I 558];

chatrībāz *m.* 'a parachutist' [BXRS I 559; McGregor 338];

churebāz *m.* 'murderer, assassin, killer' [BXRS I 569];

churebāzī *f.* 'knife-fight, knifing' [BXRS I 569];

cuhalbāz *adj.* 'merry, light-hearted, amusing, naughty' [Varma II 269; BXRS I 545; McGregor 326];

cuhalbāzī *f.* 'jollity, merriment, festivity' [Varma II 269; BXRS I 545; McGregor 326];

daṅgābāz, **daṅgebāz** *adj.* 'quarrelsome, pugnacious, turbulent, riotous'; *m.* 'a quarrelsome person' [Platts 528; BXRS I 745; McGregor 472];

dhagaṛbāz *f.* 'an adulteress' [Varma III 146; BXRS I 818; McGregor 520];

ḍhakoslebāzī *f.* 'pretence, deception, delusion' [BXRS I 675];

dhamkībāzī *f.* 'threatening behaviour, recourse to threats' [BXRS I 822; McGregor 523];

dhaṁdhlebāz *m.* 'a trickster, cheat' [BXRS I 817; McGregor 519];

dhaṁdhlebāzī *f.* 'trickery' [BXRS I 817; McGregor 519];

ḍhelebāzī, ḍhelabāzī *f.* 'the throwing of stones; stonning' [BXRS I 679; McGregor 429];

dhokhebāz *adj.* 'deceitful, fraudulent'; *m.* 'a deceitful person, an impostor' [Varma III 186; BXRS I 835; McGregor 534];

dhokhebāzī *f.* 'deceit' [Varma III 186; BXRS I 835; McGregor 534];

dillagībāz *m.* 'a joker, light-hearted person' [Varma III 67; BXRS I 780; McGregor 497];

gahrebāz *adj.* 'moving quickly (of a horse in a team)' [Varma II 90; BXRS I 454];

gahrebāzī *f.* 'quick gallop (of a harnessed horse)' [Varma II 90; BXRS I 454];

galebāz *m.* 'one who has a sweet voice, a sweet singer; boaster' [Varma II 86; BXRS I 452];

galebāzī *f.* 'sweet song; boasting' [Varma II 86; BXRS I 452];

gapbāzī, **gapoṛebāzī** *f.* 'chatter; gossips' [Varma II 72; BXRS I 446];

gapoṛebāz *m.* 'gossip; scandalmonger' [Varma II 72; BXRS I 446];

gendbāz *m.* 'bowler (cricket)' [BXRS 474; McGregor 275];

ghaplebāz *m.* 'prevaricator, trouble-maker' [Varma II 160; BXRS I 491];

ghaplebāzī *f.* 'confusion, discrepancy; fraud' [Varma II 160; BXRS I 491];

ghūṁsebāz *m.* 'a boxer' [Varma II 175; BXRS I 500; McGregor 291];

ghūṁsebāzī *f.* 'boxing' [Varma II 175; BXRS I 500; McGregor 291];

golābāzī *f.* 'a bombardment' [BXRS I 482];

gubbārebāz *m.* 'aeronaut, balloonist' [BXRS I 467];

gubbārebāzī *f.* 'aeronautics' [BXRS I 467];

guṭbāz, guṭṭabāz *m.* 'a member of faction' [BXRS I 464];

guṭbāzī, guṭṭabāzī *f.* 'factionalism' [BXRS I 464];

hullaṛbāzī *f.* 'disturbance, uproar; row' [BXRS II 819];

juebāz, juābāz *m.* 'a gambler, a gamester' [Platts 393; BXRS I 615; McGregor 376];

juebāzī *f.* 'a gambling, gamble' [BXRS I 615];

julbāz *m.* 'a cheat, trickster' [Varma II 378; BXRS I 617; McGregor 378];

julbāzī *f.* 'trickery' [Platts 386; BXRS I 617; McGregor 378];

kakkaṛbāz *m.* 'a smoker of *kakkaṛ* (cut tobacco); a *hūkka*-eater' [Platts 840; BXRS I 304];

kalābāz *m.* 'an acrobat' [Varma I 479; BXRS I 337; McGregor 178];

kalābāzī *f.* 'acrobatics, somersault' [Varma I 479; BXRS I 337; McGregor 178];

kankauebāzī *f.* 'flying kites' [BXRS I 315];

kankauvebāz *m.* 'one who is addicted to kite-flying [Platts 855];

khillībāz *adj. & m.* 'fond of joking; a joker' [Varma II 32; BXRS I 425; McGregor 238];

khillībāzī, khelbāzī *f.* 'joking' [Platts 886; BXRS I 425];

lapkebāzī *f.* 'greed' [Varma IV 559; BXRS II 495];

laṭṭhbāz *m.* 'one who wields a staff or club' [Varma IV 554; BXRS II 492; McGregor 882];

laṭṭhbāzī *f.* 'fighting with sticks or clubs' [Varma IV 554; BXRS II 492; McGregor 882];

lauṇḍebāz *m.* 'a homosexual man' [Varma IV 604; BXRS II 519; McGregor 904;];

lauṇḍebāzī *f.* 'homosexuality' [Varma IV 604; BXRS II 519; McGregor 904];

lugāībāz *m.* 'womaniser' [BXRS II 510];

lugāībāzī *f.* 'womanising' [BXRS II 510];

madakbāz *m.* 'one addicted to madak; drug addict' [BXRS II 332; McGregor 787];

maroṛbāz *m.* 'an affected person' [BXRS II 343; McGregor 793];

mukkebāz *m.* 'fist-fighter, boxer' [Varma IV 377; BXRS II 386; McGregor 819];

mukkebāzī *f.* 'boxing' [Varma IV 377; BXRS II 386; McGregor 819];

pahpaṭbāz *m.* 'brawler, trouble-maker, rowdy' [Varma III 454; BXRS II 56];

paintrebāz, paitrebāz *m.* 'one whose footwork is deft' [BXRS II 103; McGregor 645];

paintrebāzī, paitrebāzī *f.* 'knowledge of war tactics; knowledge of fencing; deftness' [BXRS II 103; McGregor 645];

pārṭībāzī *f.* 'fractional, grouped' [BXRS II 70];

pataṅgbāz *m.* 'kite-flyer' [Varma III 374; BXRS II 22; McGregor 595];

pataṅgbāzī *f.* 'kite-flying' [Varma III 374; BXRS II 22; McGregor 595];

paṭebāz *m.* 'one who plays with foils or cudgels, a fencer, a man who fights with sword and shield' [Varma III 365; BXRS II 19];

paṭebāzī *f.* 'playing with foils or cudgels, fencing' [Varma III 365; BXRS II 19];

pattharbāz *m.* 'thrower of stones' [Varma III 380; BXRS II 24; McGregor 597];

pattharbāzī *f.* 'stone- throwing' [Varma III 380; BXRS II 24; McGregor 597];

phāṭkābāz, phāṭkebāz *m.* 'speculator' [BXRS II 174; McGregor 681];

phāṭkebāzī *f.* 'speculation' [McGregor 681];

phakkaṛbāz *m.* 'an abusive, or a crude person' [Platts 287; Varma IV 2; BXRS II 162; McGregor 673];

phakkaṛbāzī *f.* 'abuse' [McGregor 637; McGregor 673];

phaṛbāz *m.* 'a gambler' [Platts 286; Varma IV 5; BXRS II 164; McGregor 675];

phaṛbāzī *f.* 'gambling' [Platts 286; BXRS II 164; McGregor 675];

phurtībāz *adj. & m.* 'active, brisk; prompt; an active, brisk person' [BXRS II 182];

posṭarbāzī *f.* 'advertising, placarding' [BXRS II 108];

raṇḍībāz *m.* 'a whoremonger' [Varma IV 457; BXRS II 442; McGregor 847];

raṇḍībāzī *f.* 'fornication' [Varma IV 457; BXRS II 442; McGregor 847];

saṭṭebāz *m.* 'a speculator' [Varma V 257; BXRS II 641; McGregor 975];

saṭṭebāzī *f.* 'a speculation Varma V 257; BXRS II 641; McGregor 975];

siṭṭībāz *m.* 'a boaster, braggart' [BXRS II 700];

suraṅgbāz *m.* 'a tunnel-digger; a mine-layer, mine-sweeper' [BXRS II 723];

suraṅgbāzī *f.* 'making a tunnel; a job of a mine-layer' [BXRS II 723];

talvārbāz *m.* 'a sword-fighter' [BXRS I 700];

talvārbāzī *f.* 'a sword-fight' [BXRS I 700];

tāṛbāz *adj.* 'of quick intelligence' [Varma II 530; BXRS I 706; McGregor 447];

tehebāz *m.* 'a conceited, prancing person; a bad man' [Varma II 577; BXRS I 729];

ṭhaṭholbāz *adj. & m.* 'jocular, facetious' [Platts 362; BXRS I 658; McGregor 410];

ṭhaṭholbāzī *f.* 'joking' [BXRS I 658; McGregor 410];

ṭhaṭṭhebāz *adj. & m.* 'jocular, facetious; a joker' [Platts 362; BXRS I 657; McGregor 410];

ṭhaṭṭhebāzī *f.* 'joking, bantering' [Platts 382; BXRS I 657; McGregor 410];

tikṛambāzī *f.* 'quibbles, intrigues, machinations' [BXRS I 713];

tiṛībāz *m.* 'cheat, swindler' [BXRS I 714];

uṛanbāz *adj.* 'flying; wandering' [BXRS I 244];

vijñāpanbāz *adj.* 'working or advertising on promotion' [BXRS II 548];

vijñāpanbāzī *f.* 'announcement, information; an advertisement' [BXRS II 548];

yojnābāz *m.* 'schemer' [BXRS II 439];

yojnābāzī *f.* '(hair-brained) scheming' [BXRS II 439];

IV. -dār(ī)

agordār *m.* 'watchman, guard' [Varma I 39; BXRS I 48];

aiṇṭhdār *adj.* 'twisted, haughty' [BXRS I 291; McGregor 144];

anīdār *adj.* 'pointed' [Varma I 102; BXRS I 85];

āpasdārī *f.* 'kinship, relationship' [Varma I 271; BXSR I 196];

aṛdār *adj.* 'stubborn' [Varma I 56; BXRS I 56];

āṛhatdār *m.* 'agent, broker, stock-broker' [Varma I 257; BXRS I 183];

baddhīdār *adj.* 'having strings, wristlets' [BXRS II 210];

bālbaccedār *adj.* 'having children' [BXRS II 243; McGregor 726];

1. **baldār** *adj.* 'strong, powerful' [Platts 163; BXRS II 219; McGregor 712];

2. **baldār** *adj.* 'twisted, coiled, bent, curved, winding (as a river), folded, wrinkled' [Platts 163; BXRS II 219; McGregor 712];

bāldār *adj.* 'hairy, shaggy; cracky (as china)' [Varma IV 119; Platts 124; BXRS II 243; McGregor 727];

bārniśdār *adj.* 'varnished' [BXRS II 240];

baṭāīdār *m.* 'a cultivator who shares the crop with the lord' [Platts 132; BXRS II 203; McGregor 699];

baṭṭedār *adj.* 'liable to discount, injured, defaced, cracked (coin etc.)' [Platts 132];

belbūṭedār, **beldār** *adj.* 'having a floral ornamentation' [Varma IV 165; BXRS II 273; McGregor 747];

bhāgdār *m.* 'a shareholder' [BXRS II 297; McGregor 763];

bhāgīdār *adj.* & *m.* 'sharing, participating' [BXRS II 297; McGregor 763];

bhāgīdārī *f.* 'participation, partnership' [BXRS II 297; McGregor 763];

bhaṛakdār *adj.* 'splendid, glittering; inspiring awe or alarm' [Varma IV 192; BXRS II 290; McGregor 758];

bharosedār *adj.* 'reliable, trustworthy' [BXRS II 293; McGregor 761];

bhaṭṭhīdār *m.* 'a distiller; keeper of a liquor-shop' [Varma IV 192; BXRS II 290; McGregor 757];

bindīdār *adj.* 'dotted, spotted' [BXRS II 248];

bisvādār *m. hist.* 'the holder of a share or shares in a village tenure' [Platts 156; Varma IV 142; BXRS II 255; McGregor 737];

bisvādārī *f.* 'tenure of shares, shared (sub-proprietary) tenure' [Platts 156; BXRS II 255; McGregor 737];

bolīdār *m.* 'a tenant holding land by verbal agreement only' [Varma IV 176; BXRS II 281; McGregor 751];

bundakīdār, **bundkīdār** *adj.* 'spotted' [Platts 169; Varma IV 148; BXRS II 259; McGregor 739];

būrdār *adj.* 'shaggy, fleecy; smelling unpleasantly' [BXRS II 264];

cakkardār *adj.* 'circular, round; circuitous; complicated' [BXRS I 508; McGregor 279];

cakledār *m.* 'the administrator and collector of revenues of a *cakla* (brothel)' [Varma I 190; BXRS I 507; McGregor 296];

calāndār *m.* 'trade-agent, shipping-clerk' [Varma II 200; BXRS I 522];

camakdār *adj.* 'glittering, gleaming, brilliant, splendid' [Varma II 207; BXRS I 515; McGregor 302];

cār<u>kh</u>ānedār *adj.* 'chequered' [McGregor 312];

caṭāīdār *adj.* 'woven' [Varma II 198; BXRS I 511; McGregor 299];

caṭakdār *adj.* 'bright, brilliant; quick, clever' [Varma II 196; BXRS I 510];

caukhṭedār *adj.* 'having a frame-work (a picture), having basement (a building)' [BXRS I 553];

cau<u>kh</u>ānedār *adj.* 'chequered, checked'; *m.* 'chequered cloth, checked muslin, cloth ornamented with squares' [BXRS I 553];

caukīdār *m.* 'a watchman, guard, local policeman' [Varma II 286; BXRS I 553; McGregor 332];

caukīdārī *f.* 'the work, position or pay of a watchman' [Varma II 286; BXRS I 553; McGregor 332];

cepdār *adj.* 'sticky, viscous' [Varma II 275; BXRS I 548; McGregor 328];

chajjedār *adj.* 'having a balcony' [Platts 460; BXRS I 558; McGregor 337];

challedār *adj.* 'having rings, or ringlets; annular, having spots of grease or oil on the surface (as soup, water)' [Varma II 302; BXRS I 562; McGregor 340];

chaṛdār *adj.* 'lattice, latticed, trellised' [BXRS I 559];

chaṛīdār *adj.* 'striped' [Varma II 296; BXRS I 559];

chatdār *adj.* 'covered, sheltered' [BXRS I 559];

chatrīdār *adj.* 'having a covering, canopy, or pavilion' [Platts 458; McGregor 338];

chāyādār *adj.* 'shaded, shady' [BXRS I 565];

cheddār *adj.* 'full of holes' [BXRS I 571];

chauldārī, **choldārī** *f.* 'a small gable tent' [Varma II 316; BXRS I 572; McGregor 349];

cittīdār *adj.* 'spotted, speckled' [Platts 424; BXRS I 533; McGregor 317];

coṭīdār *adj.* 'conical' [BXRS I 550; McGregor 330];

cunaṭdār *adj.* 'pleated, folded (cloth)' [BXRS I 542] – cf. **cunandār**;

cunandār *adj.* 'pleated, folded (cloth)' [Varma II 264; BXRS I 542] – cf. **cunaṭdār**;

cūnedār *adj.* 'of lime' [BXRS I 546];

cūṛīdār *adj.* 'gathered, drawn together into rumples or pleats' [Varma II 270; BXRS I 545; McGregor 327];

dābdār *adj.* 'powerful, mighty, awesome, oppressive' [Varma III 49; BXRS I 769; McGregor 490];

daldār *adj.* 'thick, solid, fleshy, pulpy' [Varma III 34; BXRS I 759; McGregor 157];

damakdār *adj.* 'glittering'; *fig.* 'clear, evident' [BXRS I 752; McGregor 478];

dāṁtdār *adj.* 'toothed (as a wheel), notched, having zigzag ornamentation' [BXRS I 766; McGregor 487];

ḍaṅkdār *m.* 'having a sting' [Varma II 460; BXRS I 663; McGregor 416];

dāṛhīdār *adj.* 'bearded' [BXRS; McGregor 489];

ḍauldār *adj.* 'well-built' [Varma II 478; BXRS I 674; McGregor 424];

dhabbedār *adj.* 'spotted, stained, soiled' [BXRS I 821; McGregor 523];

dhārādār *adj.* 'channelled, channel-leaved (plant)' [Platts 538];

dhārdār *adj.* 'sharp-edged' [Platts 538; BXRS I 828];

dhārīdār *adj.* 'lined, striped, streaked' [Varma III 170; BXRS I 829; McGregor 528];

dilledār *adj.* 'panelled (a door)' [Varma III 67; BXRS I 780; McGregor 497];

ḍyoṛhīdār *m.* 'door-keeper, porter' [Varma II 478; BXRS I 674; McGregor 424];

faiśandār *adj.* 'fashionable' [BXRS II 189];

gaddīdār, gaddedār *adj.* 'easy (chair)' [BXRS I 445; McGregor 254];

gāṁṭhdār *adj.* 'knotted, knotty' [Varma II 91; BXRS I 455; McGregor 261];

gaṛārīdār *adj.* 'striped, milled (a coin), zigzag (a line)' [Varma II 64; BXRS I 441; McGregor 252];

gherdār, gheredār *adj.* 'ample, roomy (of a garment)' [Platts 940; Varma II 176; BXRS I 501; McGregor 292];

ghumāvdār *adj.* 'turning, winding, spiral, complicated, tricky, over-elaborate (language)' [Varma II 173; BXRS I 499; McGregor 290];

ghuṁghrūdār *adj.* 'hung with small bells' [Varma II 170; BXRS I 498; McGregor 289];

ghuṇḍīdār *adj.* 'with buttons (cloth); decorated with buttons' [Varma II 171; BXRS I 498];

guñjdār *adj.* 'tinkling, clear, bell-like (voice)' [BXRS I 462];

jāldār *adj. & m.* 'consisting of mesh, network; a cloth or garment having network embroidery' [Varma II 362; BXRS I 604; McGregor 370];

jālīdār *adj.* 'provided with netting, netted material' [Varma II 363; BXRS I 605; McGregor 370];

jamogdār *m.* 'a person who lends a landed proprietors sum of money and recovers the loan from the tenants' [Varma II 335; BXRS I 587];

jatthedār *m.* 'a leader of a group or band' [McGregor 354];

jhāṛdār, jhāṛīdār *adj. & m.* 'having bushes, thick, dense (growth); thorny; bushy; patterned (cloth); a type of embroidery with floral ornamentation' [Varma II 408, 409; BXRS I 634];

jhāgdār *adj.* 'foaming, foamy, frothy' [BXRS I 634];

jhalakdār *adj.* 'shining, glittering' [Varma II 404; BXRS I 632];

jhālardār *adj.* 'having a fringe' [Varma II 410; BXRS I 635];

jhaṁjhrīdār *adj.* 'perforated; porous; grated, latticed' [Varma II 397; BXRS I 628];

jhaṁḍīdār *adj.* 'having a flag' [Varma II 398; McGregor 387];

jhillīdār *adj.* 'having a membrane' [Varma II 412; BXRS I 635; McGregor 395];

1. **jholdār** I *adj.* 'loose' [Varma II 420; BXRS I 639; McGregor 398];

2. **jholdār** II *adj.* 'having a juice' [Varma II 420; BXRS I 639; McGregor 398];

jhoṅkdār *adj.* 'slanting, steeped' [Varma II 419; BXRS I 638];

jhurrīdār *adj.* 'wrinkled, folded' [BXRS I 637];

joṛīdār *m.* 'a mate, partner, colleague, an equal' [Varma II 388; BXRS I 623];

jotdār *m.* 'a ploughman, tiller, one cultivating land' [Varma II 388; BXRS I 623];

kalaphdār *adj.* 'starched' [Varma I 476; BXRS I 335];

kaldār *adj.* 'having a cocking-piece (of a gun), minted (of a coin); machined'; *m.* 'a coin having a mlled edge; a rupee' [Varma I 475; BXRS I 334; McGregor 176];

kāmdār *adj.* 'worked, decorated, embroidered'; *m.* 'a manager, agent' [Varma I 512; BXRS I 355; McGregor 190];

kāṁṭedār *adj.* 'thorny, barbed (wire)' [Platts 806; BXRS I 347; McGregor 185];

kaṛākedār *adj. onom.* 'hard, strong (frost, hunger, hot)' [BXRS I 310];

kaṛīdār *adj.* 'prickly, spiny' [Varma I 439; BXRS I 311];

kaṛkdār *adj. onom.* 'crackling, crashing, growling, roaring' [BXRS I 310];

kasdār *adj.* 'active, vigorous' [Varma I 489; BXRS I 342; McGregor 181];

kaṭāvdār *adj.* 'serrated' [Varma I 434; BXRS I 308; McGregor 158];

khanakdār *adj. onom.* 'ringing, clinking, jingling' [BXRS I 412];

khevaṭdār *m.* 'tenant (of land)' [Varma II 44; BXRS I 433];

khiṛkīdār *adj.* 'having a window or having an opening (as turban)' [Platts 876; BXRS I 424; McGregor 237];

kiṭkinādār *m.* 'sub-lessee' [Varma I 528; BXRS I 366];

koṭhādār *m.* 'storeman' [Varma I 588; BXRS I 393];

kunbedār *m.* 'one who has a large family' [Platts 851];

lacakdār *adj.* 'flexible, yielding, elastic' [BXRS II 480; McGregor 881];

lahandār *m.* 'creditor, money-lender' [Varma IV 567; BXRS II 498; McGregor 889];

lahardār *adj.* 'wavy (water, a line, a pattern or hair; whimsical; crotchety; flashing, fine' [Varma IV 568; BXRS II 498; McGregor 889];

lahriyādār *adj.* 'waved; with a wave-like pattern' [Varma IV 568; BXRS II 498];

lāisensdār *m.* 'one who has a permission, licence, or patent' [BXRS II 500];

lambardār *m.* 'village headman (responsible for the government revenue)' [Varma IV 539; BXRS II 485; McGregor 877];

lambardārī *f.* 'office of headman' [McGregor 877];

lasdār *adj.* 'sticky' [Varma IV 566; BXRS II 497; McGregor 888];

laṭkedār *adj.* 'excessively elegant' [BXRS II 491];

lāvdār *adj.* 'loaded'; *m. hist.* 'cannoner' [Varma IV 578; BXRS II 505];

lendār *m.* 'a creditor; a money-lender' [Varma IV 539; BXRS II 513; McGregor 900];

locdār *adj.* 'supple, flexible, elastic' [BXRS II 517; McGregor 902];

mahakdār *adj.* 'fragrant' [Varma IV 312; BXRS II 350; McGregor 798];

malāīdār *adj.* 'creamy' [BXRS II 345; McGregor 795];

murrīdār *adj.* 'twisted' [Varma IV 395; BXRS II 396];

nākedār *adj.* & *m.* 'having an opening, a guard, a toll or custom officer' [Varma III 232; BXRS I 857; McGregor 550];

nalīdār *adj.* 'tubular' [BXRS I851];

nālīdār *adj. tech.* 'fluted, corrugated' [Varma III 251; BXRS I 865];

nātedār *adj.* & *m.* 'related; a relative' [Varma III 240; BXRS I 860; McGregor 552];

nātedārī *f.* 'relationship' [Platts 1111; BXRS I 860; McGregor 552];

pahldār *adj.* 'having sides or facets' [Varma III 455; BXRS II 56; McGregor 616];

pahredār *m.* 'a watchman, guard, sentinel' [Varma III 454; BXRS II 56; McGregor 616];

pahredārī *f.* 'watch, guard' [Varma III 454; BXRS II 56; McGregor 616];

pāldār *adj.* 'having sails (a boat)' [BXRS II 71; McGregor 625];

pāliśdār *adj.* 'polished, varnished' [BXRS II 72];

palledār *m.* 'a porter' [Varma III 447; BXRS II 53; McGregor 613];

palledārī *f.* 'the carrying of loads, a porter's work' [Varma III 447; BXRS II 53; McGregor 613];

panālīdār *adj.* 'having an outflow' [BXRS II 29];

pānīdār *adj.* 'bright, tempered (steel), respected, manly, vigorous' [Varma III 481; BXRS II 66; McGregor 623];

paratdār *adj.* 'consisting of layers' [BXRS II 33; McGregor 603];

paṭṭedār *m.* 'lease-holder, lessee' [Platts 227; BXRS II 20; McGregor 593];

paṭṭīdār, pattīdār *m.* 'holder or proprietor of a share in a coparcenary tenure of land' [Varma III 367, 379; BXRS II 20; McGregor 594];

paṭṭīdārī *f.* 'coparcenary tenure, partnership, land cultivated by coparcenary tenants, or owned jointly' [Varma III 368; BXRS II 20; McGregor 594];

pāvnedār *m.* 'a debtor, creditor' [Varma III 494; BXRS II 72];

peṭīdār *adj.* 'having tracks (a vehicle)' [BXRS II 100; McGregor 644];

phāṭakdār *m.* 'gatekeeper, pound-keeper' [Platts 282; BXRS II 174; McGregor 681];

phailāvdār *adj.* 'extensive, widely extended' [BXRS II 188; McGregor 689];

phalīdār *adj.* 'of grain legumes' [Varma IV 15; BXRS II 171];

phalītādār, phalītedār *adj.* 'having a wick, match or fuse' [BXRS II 171; McGregor 679];

pherīdār *m.* 'a vagrant, a hawker' [Platts 294;; Varma IV 33; BXRS II 187; McGregor 689];

phucṛondār *adj.* 'fringed' [BXRS II 181];

phūldār *adj.* 'having flowers, flowered (as a pattern)' [Varma IV 30; BXRS II 185; McGregor 687];

phuṁdnedār *adj.* 'decorated with a tassel' [BXRS II 181];

pūṁchdār *adj.* 'having a tail' [BXRS II 90; McGregor 640];

pūṁjīdār *m.* 'a wealthy man, a capitalist' [Varma III 549; BXRS II 91];

pūṁjīdārī *f.* 'capitalism' [Varma III 549; BXRS 91];

rasādār, rasedār *adj.* 'served with sauce (a curry)' [Varma IV 484; BXRS II 454; McGregor 856];

rasoīdār *m.* 'cook' [Varma IV 487; BXRS II 455; McGregor 857];

rasoīdārī *f.* 'cooking, cookery' [Varma IV 487; BXRS II 455; McGregor 857];

ravedār *adj.* 'granulated' [Varma IV 479; BXRS II 452; McGregor 854];

royendār *adj.* 'hairy, woolly, furred' [BXRS II 483; McGregor 873];

rūīdār *adj.* 'padded, quilted with cotton' [Varma IV 519; BXRS II 473; McGregor 868];

sajdār *adj.* 'handsome; elegant' [Varma V 254; BXRS II 639; McGregor 974];

sājhedār *m.* 'a partner, associate, a shareholder' [Varma V 333; BXRS II 685; McGregor 1003;];

sājhedārī *f.* 'partnership' [Varma V 333; BXRS II 685; McGregor 1003];

sansanīdār *adj.* 'causing a thrill, exciting, sensational' [McGregor 980];

senādār *m.* '19 c. commander, general' [Varma V 445; BXRS II 739; McGregor 1038];

sevādār *m.* 'a servant in a Sikh gurudvara' [Varma V 448; BXRS II 741];

sevārdār *adj.* 'covered with water-plants' [BXRS I 742];

spriṅgdār *adj.* 'having a spring' [BXRS II 762];

surdār *adj.* 'resonant; of a beautiful voice' [Varma V 412; BXRS II 724];

tanāvdār *adj.* 'stretched, pulled tight' [BXRS I 689];

tanīdār *adj.* 'having strings' [Varma II 503; BXRS I 690; McGregor 437];

taṛapdār *adj.* 'flashing, glittering' [Varma II 498; BXRS 686];

tehedār *m.* 'a conceited, prancing person; a bad man' [Varma II 577; BXRS I 729];

thailīdār *m.* & *adj.* 'one who holds money, a banker, cashier, treasurer' [Varma III 9; BXRS I 744; McGregor 471];

thailedār *m.* 'a rich, wealthy man' [BXRS I 744] – cf. **thailī-śāh.**

thāṁgīdārī *f.* 'the aiding and abetting of thieves; the receiving or holding of stolen goods' [Varma III 4; BXRS I 741];

thandār *adj.* 'having an udder, a large udder; in milk' [Platts 348; BXRS I 739; McGregor 468];

thānedār *m.* 'a police sergeant, superintendent of a police or station post' [Varma III 5; BXRS I 741; McGregor 469];

thānedārī *f.* & *adj.* 'the position or rank of *thānedār* having to do with position of *thānedār*' [Varma III 5; BXRS I 741; McGregor 469];

ṭhāṭhdār *adj.* 'lovely, splendid' [BXRS I 660];

ṭhasakdār *adj.* 'haughty, vain, ostentatious' [Varma II 451; BXRS I 658];

ṭhīkedār, hekedār *m.* 'a contractor' [Varma II 455, 457; BXRS I 661; McGregor 413];

thokdār *m.* 'a wholesale dealer' [Varma III 9; BXRS I 744; McGregor 471];

ṭoṇṭīdār *adj.* 'having a spout' [Platts 360; BXRS I 653; McGregor 407];

ṭopīdār *adj.* 'wearing a hat' [Varma II 444; BXRS I 654; McGregor 407];

toṛedār *f. hist.* 'having a match (a matchlock)' [Platts 342; BXRS I 731; McGregor 463];

ubhārdār *adj.* 'prominent, raised; relief (map)' [Varma I 375; BXRS I 272; McGregor 131];

uljhandār *adj.* 'tangled; intricate' [BXRS I 274; McGregor 132];

V. -faroś

bātfaroś *m.* 'seller of tales, romancer' [BXRS II 237; McGregor 723];

gudṛīfaroś *m.* 'a second-hand clothes seller' [BXRS I 466];

thokfaroś *m.* 'a wholesale dealer' [BXRS I 744; McGregor 471];

VI. -gīr(-ā)

āṛgīr *m.* 'partition, bulkhead; balk, boundary strip' [Varma I 256; BXRS I 182];

bāggīr *m.* 'a groom, stableman' [Platts 123; BXRS II 232];

chatgīr *m.* 'a roof; bed-curtain' [Varma II 296; BXRS I 559];

chatgīrī *f.* 'ceiling (made of cloth); bed-curtain' [Varma II 296; BXRS I 559];

gacgīr *m.* 'plasterer' [BXRS I 439];

rājgīr *m.* 'a mason, builder (properly a master-mason)' [Varma IV 493; BXRS II 458; McGregor 860];

uṭhāīgīr *m.* 'a pilferer, petty thief; a rascal' [Varma I 328; BXRS I 243; McGregor 117];

uṭhāīgīrā *m.* 'a pilferer, petty thief; a rascal' [Varma I 328; BXRS I 243; McGregor 117];

VI. -girī, -gīrī

bābūgirī *f. pej.* 'pettiness of outlook or conduct' [BXRS II 239; McGregor 725];

baṛhaīgirī *f.* 'carpentering, carpenter's work' [BXRS II 205];

bairāgīrī *f.* 'waiter's duties' [BXRS II 278];

cāṁciyāgirī *f.* 'stealing, theft, robbery' [Varma II 225; BXRS I 523];

chatgīrī *f.* 'a ceiling-cloth' [Platts 458; Varma II 296; BXRS I 559];

dādāgirī *f. pej.* 'bullying, loutish behaviour' [BXRS I 768; McGregor 489];

dāīgirī *f.* 'midwifery, a nurse's duties' [BXRS I 767; McGregor 488];

dhobīgirī *f.* 'the washerman's trade' [BXRS I 836; McGregor 534];

gacgīrī *f.* 'plastering; building, brick-laying' [Platts 458; Varma II 296; BXRS I 439];

guṇḍāgirī *f.* 'meanness, baseness' [BXRS I 462];

machuāgirī *f.* 'fishing (an occupation)' [BXRS II 326; McGregor 783];

mukhiyāgirī *f.* 'leadership' [BXRS II 388];

netāgīrī *f. pej.* 'leadership, leader's position or status' [Varma III 323; BXRS I 901; McGregor 580];

ojhāīgīrī *f.* 'the practice of sorcery' [BXRS I 294; McGregor 146];

paṭvārgirī *f.* 'the office or duties of a *paṭvārī* (registrar of a village's land accounts)' [Varma III 363; BXRS II 18; McGregor 592];

rājgīrī *f.* 'mason's or builder's work or occupation masonry' [Varma IV 493; BXRS II 458; McGregor 860];

uṭhāīgīrī *f.* 'theft, dirty trick' [BXRS I 243];

VII. -kaś(ī)

ārākaś *m.* 'a sawyer' [Varma I 281; BXRS I 205; McGregor 92];

chīṁṭākaśī *f.* 'casting aspersions, ridiculing' [BXRS I 568; McGregor 345];

dhuāṁkaś *m.* 'flue, chimney, funnel, smoke-stuck' [Varma III 175; BXRS I 830];

gondkaś *m.* 'a gum- or glue-brush' [Platts 927; BXRS I 477];

jhāṛūkaś *m.* 'a sweeper' [Platts 400; BXRS I 634];

kandlākaś *m.* 'a master preparing a gold or silver wire' [Varma I 423; BXRS I 302];

kandlākaśī *f.* 'producing a gold or silver wire' [Varma I 423];

phalīkaś *m.* 'a hook for drawing the looped strings through the holes by which the walls of a tent are laced to the top' [Platts 289];

phāṁkākaśī *f.* 'hunger, starvation' [BXRS II 173];

rassākaśī *f.* 'tug-of-war' [Varma IV 487; BXRS II 455; McGregor 857];

VIII. -k͟hānā

bahlk͟hānā *m.* 'a place for carts' [BXRS II 224; McGregor 715];

baiṭhakk͟hānā *m.* 'a sitting room' [BXRS II 276; McGregor 748];

bhaṭhīyārk͟hānā *m.* also *pej.* 'inn; eating-house' [Varma IV 192; BXRS II 290; McGregor 757];

bhaṁgerk͟hānā *m.* 'a shop or a place where *bhāṁg* is sold or drunk' [BXRS II 286; McGregor 754];

bhūtk͟hānā *m.* *colloq.* 'fiends' house; dirty or neglected living quarters' [Varma IV 232; BXRS II 309; McGregor 771];

būcaṛk͟hānā *m.* 'a slaughter-house' [Varma IV 154; BXRS II 264];

caklāk͟hānā *m.* 'brothel' [BXRS I 507];

caṇḍūk͟hānā *m.* 'an opium-smokers' den' [Varma II 183; BXRS I 504];

cārk̲h̲ānā, **cauk̲h̲ānā** *adj.* 'chequered, checked; consisting of lines intersecting at right angles (a design)'; *m.* 'chequered cloth, checked muslin, cloth ornamented with squares; the four points of the compass; the four quarters of the world; on all sides' [Varma II 232, 286; BXRS I 527; McGregor 312, 331];

chāpāk̲h̲ānā *m.* 'a printing firm, printing works' [Varma II 305; BXRS I 553; McGregor 342];

ciṛiyāk̲h̲ānā *m.* 'aviary, zoo' [Varma II 243; BXRS I 532; McGregor 316];

cork̲h̲ānā *m.* 'a hiding place, secret pigeon-hole (in a drawer)' [Varma II 281; BXRS I 551];

dhobīk̲h̲ānā *m.* 'a laundry (= *dhobīghar*)' [BXRS I 836; McGregor 534];

gāṛīk̲h̲ānā *m.* 'a carriage-house, coach-house; a cab-stand' [Varma II 94; BXRS I 456];

hāthīk̲h̲ānā *m.* 'an elephant's house or stable; elephant-shed' [Platts 1215; Varma V 542; BXRS II 805; McGregor 1069];

juāk̲h̲ānā, **jūāk̲h̲ānā**, **jūek̲h̲ānā** *m.* 'a gambling-house' [Platts 394; Varma II 380; BXRS I 615; McGregor 376];

kabāṛk̲h̲ānā *m.* 'lumber-room; scrap-merchant's shop or premises' [Varma I 453; BXRS I 319];

kalālk̲h̲ānā, **kalvārk̲h̲ānā** *m.* 'liquor-shop, drinking-house' [Varma I 480; BXRS I 337; McGregor 177];

karañjk̲h̲ānā *m.* 'hen-house' [Varma I 459; BXRS I 325];

katvārk̲h̲ānā *m.* 'scrap-heap, a rubbish-dump' [Varma I 441; BXRS I 312];

kūṛāk̲h̲ānā *m.* 'public rubbish-dump' [Varma I 570; BXRS I 385; McGregor 211];

lohārkhānā *m.* 'a smithy' [Varma IV 603; BXRS II 519; McGregor 903];

mistrīkhānā *m.* 'workshop' [Varma IV 365; BXRS II 378; McGregor 814];

moṭarkhānā *m.* 'a garage' [BXRS II 414];

modīkhānā *m.* 'a grocer's or merchant's shop, store' [Varma IV 422; BXRS II 416; McGregor 836];

pothīkhānā *m.* 'a library, book-depository' [BXRS II 107; McGregor 648];

raṇḍīkhānā *m.* 'a brothel' [Varma IV 457; BXRS II 442; McGregor 847];

rasoīkhānā *m.* 'kitchen' [Varma IV 487; BXRS II 455];

tāṛīkhānā *m.* 'an inn where palm-wine is served' [BXRS I 706];

IX. -khor(-ā, -ī)

akalkhurā *adj.* 'proud, haughty, egoist' [Platts 66; Varma I 26; BXRS I 41];

byāzkhor *m.* 'interest-eater: a money lender' [Varma IV 178; BXRS II 282; McGregor 751];

byāzkhorī *f.* 'usury' [BXRS II 282; McGregor 751];

ghamkhor *adj.* 'greenhouse (plant)' [Varma II 160; BXRS I 491];

ghūskhor *m.* 'one who takes bribes' [Varma II 176; BXRS I 501; McGregor 291];

ghūskhorī *f.* 'bribery, bribe-taking' [Varma II 176; BXRS I 501];

jūtākhor, jūtīkhor *adj. & m. pej.* 'beaten with shoes, mean base, one who has suffered a shoe-beating' [Varma II 381; BXRS I 619; McGregor 379];

lagānkhorī *f.* 'a time for paying the rent for land' [BXRS II 488];

latkhor, latkhorā *adj.* 'kicked'; *fig.* 'contemptible; a contemptible person; mat (for the feet)' [Varma IV 557; BXRS II 493; McGregor 884];

mailkhorā *adj. & m.* 'dark or dull coloured; an overall; undergarment; saddle-pad' [Varma IV 418; BXRS II 413; McGregor 834];

māṁskhor *adj.* 'meat-eating' [Varma IV 331; BXRS II 359; McGregor 802];

peṁśankhor *adj.* 'having a pension, pensioned' [BXRS II 98];

ṭukṛekhor, ṭukaṛkhor *m.* 'one who lives on or who devours scraps or livings; one who sponges; a dependant' [Platts 357; BXRS I 649];

udhārkhor *m.* 'one who lives on borowings' [BXRS I 259];

yuddhkhor *m.* 'war-monger' [BXRS II 434];

X. -navīs(ī)

ciṭnavīs *m. hist.* 'writer' [Varma II 241; BXRS I 531];

kāpīnavīs *m.* 'a copyist' [Varma I 509; BXRS I 353];

ṭillenavīsī *f. pej.* 'frivolous, or degrading activity' [Varma II 435; BXRS I 648; McGregor 404];

XI. -nigar

kārṭūnnigār *m.* 'cartoonist' [BXRS I 357];

XII. -niśīn, -naśīn

gaddīniśīn *adj.* 'the incumbent of a seat of office; a regent, vice-regent' [Varma II 71; BXRS I 445; McGregor 254];

gaddīniśīnī *f.* 'accession to office' [BXRS I 445; McGregor 254];

godnaśīn *m.* 'adopted child' [BXRS I 479];

godnaśīnī *f.* 'adoption' [BXRS I 479];

rāsnaśīn, rāsniśīn *adj.* 'adopted (a son)' [BXRS II 466; McGregor 863];

sattaniśīn *adj.* 'established in power' [McGregor 977];

XIII. -numā

gendnumā *adj.* 'spherical' [BXRS I 474];

guthlīnumā *adj.* 'baggy' [BXRS I 466];

sīṛhīnumā *adj. inv.* 'formed like a flight of steps, terraced' [Varma V 379; BXRS II 712; McGregor 1020];

XIV. -parast(ī)

faiśanparast *adj.* 'fashionable'; *m.* 'dandy, coxcomb' [BXRS II 189];

faiśanparastī *f.* 'following the fashion' [BXRS II 189];

kunbāparastī *f.* 'attachment to family life' [BXRS I 377];

phūṭparast *adj.* 'schismatic, dissenting'; *m. hist.* 'schismatic, dissenter' [BXRS II 184];

phūṭparastī *f.* 'splitting tactics' [BXRS II 184];

pūṁjīparast *adj.* 'capitalist'; *m.* 'one devoted to wealth' [BXRS II 91];

samjhautāparast *adj. & m.* 'opportunist; compromiser' [Varma V 278; BXRS II 653];

samjhautāparastī *f.* 'opportunism; compromise' [Varma V 278; BXRS II 653];

sāmrājyaparast *adj.* 'imperial' [BXRS II 692];

śāntiparast *m.* 'pacifist' [BXRS II 594];

XV. -poś

cilampoś *m.* 'the lid of a cilam' [Varma II 255; McGregor 320];

khapṛailpoś *adj.* 'tiled (roof)' [BXRS I 413];

palaṅgpoś *m.* 'coverlet' [Varma III 441; BXRS II 51; McGregor 611];

XVI. -rasān

ciṭṭhīrasān *m.* 'deliverer of a letter, postman' [Varma II 242; BXRS I 532; McGregor 315];

XVII. -sāz(ī)

bidarsāz *m.* 'maker of bidar vessels, silver-plater' [Platts 140; BXRS II 251; McGregor 732];

bijlīsāz *m.* 'electrician, electrical engineer' [BXRS II 250];

dāṁtsāz *m.* 'dental technician, dentist' [BXRS I 766; McGregor 487];

ghaṛīsāz *m.* 'a watchmaker' [Varma II 157; BXRS I 490; McGregor 284];

ghaṛīsāzī *f.* 'a watchmaker's trade or craft' [Varma II 157; BXRS I 490; McGregor 284];

kanghīsāz *m.* 'a small comb' [BXRS I 300];

membarsāzī *f.* 'the fixing or making of boundaries; a record of boundaries' [Varma IV 409; BXRS II 407; McGregor 831];

pannīsāz *m.* 'a craftsman making tinsel, tin-foil' [Varma III 393; BXRS II 30];

pannīsāzī *f.* 'production of tinsel, tin-foil' [Varma III 393; BXRS II 30];

XVIII. -śāh(ī)

abhijātśāhī *f.* 'nobles' oligarchy; government of aristocracy' [BXRS I 113];

baiṅkśāh *m.* 'financier' [BXRS II 276];

bālūśāhī *f.* 'a sweet consisting of pastries fried in ghī, dipped in molasses or syrup and sprinkled with sugar' [Platts 125; Varma IV 121; BXRS II 245; McGregor 728];

baniyāśāhī *f.* 'plutocracy' [BXRS II 212];

ḍaṇḍāśāhī *f.* 'discipline of the mailed feast' [BXRS I 664];

guṇḍāśāhī *adj.* 'of hooligan' [BXRS I 462];

mahājanśāhī *f.* 'a financial oligarchy' [BXRS II 352];

netāśāhī *f.* 'supreme position or status as leader' [BXRS I 901; McGregor 580];

popśāhī *f.* 'a Pope's authority' [BXRS II 107];

pūṁjīśāhī *adj.* & *f.* 'capitalist, capitalism' [BXRS II 91; McGregor 640];

rājśāhī *f.* 'royal status, royalty' [McGregor 860];

sāmantśāhī *f.* 'rule through feudatories; the feudal system' [Varma V 342; BXRS II 690; McGregor 1004];

sāmrājyaśāhī *f.* 'imperialism' [BXRS II 692; McGregor 1007];

samrāṭśāhī *f.* 'monarchy' [BXRS II 664];

sattaśāhī *f.* 'dictatorship' [BXRS II 643];

tānāśāh *m.* 'a despot, dictator' [Varma II 532; BXRS I 708; McGregor 448];

tānāśāhī *f.* 'despotism' [Varma II 532; BXRS I 708; McGregor 448];

thailīśāh *m.* 'a rich, wealthy man' [BXRS I 744] – cf. **thailedār**;

thailīśāhī *f.* & *adj.* 'plutocratic; plutocracy' [BXRS I 744].

ṭhākurśāhī *f.* 'dominance of the landed class' [BXRS I 659; McGregor 411];

APPENDIX II

INDEX OF CITED WORDS AND FORMATIVES